ELEMENTARY
coursebook

Lindsay Clandfield

Kate Pickering

with additional material by Amanda Jeffries

MACMILLAN

About Global

Lindsay Clandfield is a teacher, teacher educator and lead author of Global. He was born in England, grew up in Canada, taught at a university in Mexico, lives in Spain and has trained teachers from around the world. He is also the creator of the popular blog **Six Things** (www.sixthings.net), a collection of lists about ELT.

Kate Pickering is the Director of the Adults' department at International House Madrid. There she combines running a large department with her work as a teacher trainer and assessor on Cambridge CELTA and DELTA as well as IH's in-service training programmes. She continues to teach regularly and particularly enjoys working with low level students such as the senior learners she taught while writing Global Elementary.

Six things we wanted for global

real lives

international voices

intellectual curiosity

cultural knowledge

a global outlook

a different book

Global Elementary by numbers:

10 units   160 pages   37 texts about people & places   49 vocabulary sections   34 explanations of English grammar   10 functional English lessons   27 accents from around the world in Global Voices   260 audio clips   30 video clips   150 interactive activities   100s of curious and interesting facts

Content highlights

1 Facts & Figures
Global English facts Number plates from around the world The power of numbers Telecommunications facts and figures in the UK and the US

2 Where & When
Megacities Created capitals The cross-border commuter Calendars from around the world

3 Family & Friends
Shakespeare's tragic families Scottish clans Meeting places around the world
Man's best friend ... people and dogs in history

4 Bed & Breakfast
Hotels with a difference Couchsurfing ... a new way to travel A full English breakfast *Hungry Planet* ... an interview with Peter Menzel

5 Film & Television
World cinema Make a pitch ... great ideas for films Television theories ... the effects of television on human beings Film reviews

6 Work & Study
The Gallup survey of young people Ten facts about typing Important firsts ... centres of learning School days

7 News & Weather
The news ... from local to global *All the President's Men* by Woodward & Bernstein The great Eskimo vocabulary hoax Storm chasing: a great day out?

8 Coming & Going
Pedal Power Coming to Hong Kong The four stages of culture shock Why did you go? Four people who emigrated

9 Life & Style
One planet, one place! ... the Encyclopedia of Life Rites of passage The history of fashion ... the origins of seven common items

10 Fun & Games
Masters of fun Malta fact file A ball can change the world ... The Homeless World Cup Kim's Game

Global English
by David Crystal

Contents

EV - Extend your vocabulary (P) - Pronunciation

Reading

1 What do you know about the English language? Work in pairs. Guess the answers.

1 English is the official language in …
   a 20 countries.
   b 50 countries.
   c more than 50 countries.
2 English is a first (1st) or second (2nd) language for more than …
   a 5 billion people.
   b 50 million people.
   c 500 million people.
3 Many English words are not new for beginner English students because …
   a they are similar in other languages.
   b they are from the world of business, travel, fashion and music.
   c both of the above (a and b).

2 🔊 1.01 Read and listen to *Global English Facts* and check your guesses.

Global English facts

English is the first or second language for more than 500 million people in the world.

English is an official language in more than 50 countries.

Many English words are not new to beginner English students. There are three reasons for this:

• There are many international words in English. These words are the same in many different languages. *Doctor* and *radio* are international words.

• Many English words are similar in other languages. *Policía* (Spanish), *polizei* (German), *police* (French), *polizia* (Italian) and *police* (English) are all similar.

• People know a lot of English because it is connected to the world of music, travel, business, fashion or computers. For example, *email, hotel*.

Vocabulary

1 Look at the *A to Z of global English*. Match the words to the categories in the box below.

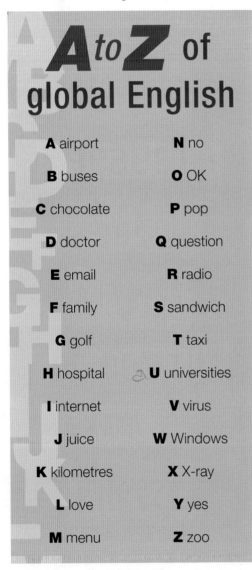

A to Z of global English

A airport	**N** no
B buses	**O** OK
C chocolate	**P** pop
D doctor	**Q** question
E email	**R** radio
F family	**S** sandwich
G golf	**T** taxi
H hospital	**U** universities
I internet	**V** virus
J juice	**W** Windows
K kilometres	**X** X-ray
L love	**Y** yes
M menu	**Z** zoo

computers   expressions
food and drink   jobs   music   places
sports   transport   other

2 🔊 1.02 Listen and check your answers.

3 Work in pairs. Think of other words for these categories. Then compare with other pairs.

Grammar

an airport, airport*s*
a doctor, doctor*s*
a family, famil*ies*
a sandwich, sandwich*es*

- use *a* / *an* with singular nouns
- use *a* with a consonant sound and use *an* with a vowel sound
- plural nouns are formed with *s* / *es* / *ies*

1 Look at the alphabet again and find examples of …

1 *an* + noun.   2 *a* + noun.   3   plural nouns.

2 Write *a* or *an*.

__ alphabet		__ director		__ hotel	
__ bus		__ email		__ pizza	
__ computer		__ football		__ telephone	

3 Add any new words from exercise 2 to the categories in vocabulary exercise 1.

G **Grammar focus** – explanation & more practice of articles on page 136

Pronunciation

1 🔊 1.03 Listen and repeat the letters and words in the alphabet.

2 🔊 1.04 Listen to how English letters are pronounced.

/eɪ/	/iː/	/e/	/aɪ/	/əʊ/	/uː/	/ɑː/
A	B	F	I	O	Q	R
H	C	L	Y		W	
J	D	N			U	
K	G	X				
	P	Z				
	V	M S				
	T					

3 Complete the table with these letters.

E   K   M   S   T   U   Y

4 🔊 1.05 Listen and check your answers. Then repeat the letters.

5 Work in pairs. A: spell a word from the *A to Z of global English*. B: point to the word. Then swap roles.

Facts & Figures

Vocabulary and Speaking

1 Put the letters in the correct order to spell the numbers.

0	eozr	3	reeht	6	xis	9	einn
1	noe	4	rouf	7	vesne	10	net
2	wot	5	evif	8	theig		

2 Work in pairs. Turn to page 130. Practise saying letters and numbers.

Listening *say them first*

1 Work in pairs. Look at the number plates. Can you guess where they come from? Use the countries in the box below to help you.

Afghanistan	Austria	Canada
Ghana	Korea	Ireland	Italy
Mexico	Russia	US

Useful phrases

- What about this one?
- Is it from Ireland?
- Yes.
- No. It's from Italy.

2 🔊 1.06–1.07 Listen to two conversations. Match the number plate to the conversation.

1- 259 HFY   2- ACHT 713

3 Do you have a car? What is the number plate? Tell a partner.

The number plate is …

I don't have a car.

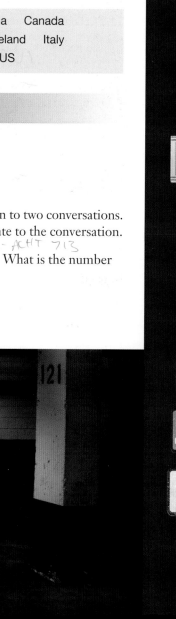

Number plates from around the world

ONTARIO
ACHT ♛ 713
YOURS TO DISCOVER

RT3963P GH

ش ٦١٢ كابل
KBL 232 SH

729-PLA
DISTRITO FEDERAL

A **NT ✠ 83 JO**

i **CF 796FW**

TEXAS
259★HFY

京 H **L 7987**

GAILLIMH
IRL **18-G-03215**

H142 BT **88** RUS

Grammar

> *I'm Mr Forbes.*
> *It **isn't** my car.*
> ***Is** it the red car? No, it **isn't**.*

- we use contractions in speaking and informal writing
- we don't use contractions in formal writing

1 Circle the correct form of the verb in the two conversations. Then listen again and check your answers.

Conversation 1

A: Hi. I'm Mr Forbes – *I'm* / *I is* here for my car.

B: Mr John Forbes?

A: Yes, that's right.

B: *Is* / *are* your car the BMW?

A: Yes.

B: *Is it* / *It's* over here.

A: But this isn't my car.

B: Sorry?

A: *It not* / *It isn't* my car. My car license plate *is* / *am* 259 HFY.

B: Oh ...

Conversation 2

A: Hello, we *is* / *are* here for the car.

B: Your names please?

A: John and Lisa Thomson.

B: Ah yes, the Ford Focus.

A: That's right.

B: *Is the car* / *The car is* in the car park. Number plate ACHT 713.

A: Is it the red car?

B: No it isn't. *It's* / *They're* the blue Focus over there. Here's the key.

A: OK. Thanks.

2 Complete the world number plate facts with *is* or *are*.

Language note: a *number plate* is called a *license plate* in American English.

World number plate facts

Number plates _____ a combination of numbers and letters.

In the USA, the number plate _____ different in each state.

In Russia, taxi number plates _____ yellow and black.

In Pakistan, all number plates _____ in the Latin alphabet.

Number plates _____ on the front and back of a car.

A personalised number plate _____ a special plate with words or a phrase.

In Britain, number plates _____ different colours at the front and back. They _____ white on the front and yellow at the back.

G **Grammar focus –**
explanation & more practice of the verb *be* on page 136

Speaking

Work in pairs. Choose **one** of the tasks below.

A Practise saying the number plates. A: say a number. B: point to the correct number plate.

B Choose one of the conversations from Grammar exercise 1. Read the conversation together. Then close your books and practise the conversation again.

C Choose one of the conversations from Grammar exercise 1, but change the information (name, car, number plate, etc). Try to memorise as much as you can. Then practise the conversation.

Vocabulary

1 Put these numbers in the correct order.

- eleven
- fifteen
- twenty
- eighteen
- twelve
- fourteen
- seventeen
- nineteen
- thirteen
- sixteen

2 1.08 Listen and check your answers.

3 Write the numbers for the words.

1 twenty-one
2 thirty
3 forty-six
4 fifty-five
5 sixty-nine
6 seventy-seven
7 eighty
8 ninety-three

4 1.09 Listen and circle the correct number.

1 (13)   30
2 (15)   50
3 17   (70)
4 19   (90)
5 (14)   40
6 16   (60)
7 (18)   80

Reading

1 You are going to read a text about numbers. Check you understand these words.

| common | lucky | sequence | unlucky |

2 1.10 Read and listen to *The power of numbers* on page 11 and find an example of …

1 a common number in religion.
2 a lucky number.
3 an unlucky number.
4 a number in a sequence.

3 Work in pairs. Ask each other these questions.

- Are there special numbers in your culture? What are they?
- Do you have a lucky / unlucky number? What is it?

Listening and Vocabulary

1 1.11 Read and listen to these ordinal numbers.

1st	first
2nd	second
3rd	third
4th	fourth
5th	fifth
6th	sixth
7th	seventh
8th	eighth
9th	ninth
10th	tenth

Language note: use ordinal numbers to say the order or sequence of things or to say the date.
the first, the second, the third, etc
9th February

2 1.12 Read and listen to *One, two, three, five, eight …* on page 11. What are the sixth, seventh and eighth numbers in the sequence?

Listening and Speaking

1 1.13 Listen and write the numbers.

2 1.14 Work in pairs. What are the next two numbers in each sequence? Listen and check your answers.

Useful phrases

- The next number is …
- I think it's …
- Maybe it's …

3 Create another sequence and tell your partner. Can they guess the next two numbers in the sequence?

The power of numbers

Eight

In China, the number 8 is lucky. The word for 8 is similar to the word for rich.

Three

3 is a very common number in mathematics, science, religion, education and politics.

Thirteen

For many people in America and Western Europe, 13 is an unlucky number. In many hotels there is no room 13. On Continental Airlines, Air France, KLM and Iberia there is no row 13.

SEPTEMBER
FRIDAY
13

Boss: the man who is early when you are late, and late when you are early.

One, two, three, five, eight ...

This is a sequence of numbers, called Fibonacci numbers.

The first number in the sequence is 1

The second number is 2.   **1, 2**

The third number is the first number plus the second number.   **1, 2, 3**

The fourth number is the second number plus the third number.   **1, 2, 3, 5**

Fibonacci numbers are common in nature.

Facts & Figures

Part 4

Reading and listening

1 🔊 **1.15** Read and listen to *Telecommunication facts and figures*. Are the sentences true (T) or false (F)?

1 The words for portable phone in Britain and the US are different. T
2 Britain has more fixed phones per 100 people than the US. +
3 The emergency number in Britain and the US starts with the number nine. T
4 The freephone numbers are the same. f
5 The information number in Britain and the US is the same. f

2 What important telephone numbers do you know in your country? *number for France?*

Extend your vocabulary – *about*

Use *about* before a number when it is not exact.
In the US it is about 85 per 100 people.
This mobile phone is €59.99.

Look at the sentences and add *about* if it is possible.
1 Our teacher is 35.
2 The station is ten minutes from the school.
3 In China, 8 is a lucky number.
4 The number before 12 is 11.

Vocabulary

1 🔊 **1.16** Listen and repeat these email and website addresses.
jenny@britmail.co.uk
baxter21@phonemail.net
www.bbc.co.uk
www.independent.co.uk/sport

2 How do we pronounce these symbols?
1 @
2 .
3 www
4 /

3 Work in pairs. A: turn to page 126. B: turn to page 128. Practise saying some email and website addresses.

The UK and US ... telecommunication facts and figures

In the UK, the number of mobile phones is about 118 per 100 people.
In the US it is about 85 per 100 people.

The emergency number for the police, ambulance and fire department is 999 in the UK.

In the US it is 911.

The international phone code for the UK is 44. For the US it is 1.

In the UK, freephone numbers begin with 080. In the US they begin with 1-800 or 1-888.

A portable phone is called different things. In the UK it is called a *mobile phone* and in the US it is called a *cell phone*.

The number of fixed telephone lines per 100 people in the UK is 55 out of 100. In the US it is 53 out of 100.

The information number (the number to find other numbers) is 118 in the UK. In the US it is 411.

Listening

1 🔊 **1.17–1.18** Listen to two conversations. Match a picture a–c to the correct conversation. There is one picture you do not need.

1 = b   2 = c

2 Listen again and complete the information.

> Name: Mr & Mrs Steinbeck
> Nights: 2
> Telephone: 0044 1845705886
> Email: peter.steinbeck@blc.net
> Room: 224

> **Name:** Lisa Morley
> **Contact telephone:** 0120267110
> **Address:** 15 Bedford Road, Bedford

Grammar

> *My* name's Steinbeck.
> What's *your* telephone number?
> Here's *their* key.
>
> - use possessive adjectives such as *my* and *your* before a noun
> - use *your* for both singular and plural

1 Rewrite the sentences so they mean the same.

I'm Lucy.   *My name's Lucy.*
1 You're Keyi.
2 His name's Paolo.
3 She's Brigitte.
4 Our names are Bernard and Julie.
5 They're Pablo and Luis.

a

b

c

2 🔊 **1.19** Read a dialogue between a student and a receptionist at a language school. Underline the correct option. Then listen and check your answers.

S = Student   **R** = Receptionist

S: Good morning. *I'm* / My Sergei Andropov and this is I / *my* wife Katya.

R: Hello – welcome to International English. I / *My* name's Antonia. You / *Your* teacher is Don Miller. *He's* / His from Australia. *You're* / Your in classroom 6.

S: Thank you.

ⓖ **Grammar focus** – explanation & more practice of possessive adjectives on page 136

Speaking

Work in pairs. Ask each other questions to find out your partner's …

- name.
- address.
- phone number.
- email.

Function globally meeting people

| a | In a café | b | At an airport | c | In a hospital | d | At a taxi rank |

Warm up

Work in pairs. Do you remember the names of other people in the class? Take it in turns to introduce them.

> ### Useful phrases
>
> - His name is …
> - Her name is …
> - This is …
> - That is …

Listening

1 🔊 **1.20–1.23** Listen to four conversations. Match each one to a picture. Which conversations are formal (F) and which ones are informal (I)?

2 Listen again and choose the correct option.

Conversation 1: The man and woman *are* / *aren't* friends.
Conversation 2: It *is* / *isn't* her first day.
Conversation 3: The man and the woman *are* / *aren't* in the taxi together.
Conversation 4: The *second* / *third* man is Mr Brown.

3 Read the audioscript on page 152 and check your answers.

Language focus: meeting people

1 Put the words in the correct order to make phrases.

1 meet you pleased to.
2 OK, I'm thanks.
3 going how's it?

2 Complete the table with the phrases from exercise 1.

Hello.	Nice to meet you.	I'm fine, thank you.	My name's …	How are you?
Hi. Hey.	———— Good to see you.	Fine, thanks. ————	I'm …	————

> **Language note:** use *Good to see you* when you meet a friend, **not** when you meet someone for the first time.

3 Tick (✔) the more formal expressions in the table.

Speaking

Work in pairs. Choose **one** of the tasks below.

A Look at the audioscript on page 152. Read the conversations together. Choose one conversation and try to memorise it. Then practise it.

B Look at the audioscript on page 152. Write similar formal and informal conversations. Then practise them.

Global voices

Warm up

1 Think of five well-known people from different countries. Write their names and where they are from.

2 Work in pairs. Tell your partner about the people you wrote.

His name is … He's from …
Her name is … She's from …

Listening

1 🔊 **1.24–1.33** Listen to ten people saying their names and where they are from. Tick (✔) the places you hear.

Austria	China	Germany	Italy	Mexico
Moscow	Rome	Russia	Saudi Arabia	
Switzerland	Tokyo	Ukraine		

Aki Menahi Christina
Hani Elodie Liliya
Sara Maxim Amy

2 Listen again and complete the information about each speaker.

Speaker 1: Aki from _____
Speaker 2: Menahi from _____
Speaker 3: Christina from _____
Speaker 4: Hani from _____, from _____
Speaker 5: Elodie from _____, from _____
Speaker 6: Liliya from _____
Speaker 7: Sara from _____
Speaker 8: Maxim from _____, from _____
Speaker 9: Elizabeth from _____
Speaker 10: Amy from _____

Language focus: talking about where you are from

Look at the different ways the speakers say where they are from. Make similar sentences about yourself.

- I'm from Tokyo.
  I'm from …
- I come from Russia.
  I come from …
- I am from Saudi Arabia, I am from Riyadh. Riyadh is the capital of Saudi Arabia.
  I am from …, I am from …
- I come from Switzerland, from Geneva.
  I come from …, from …
- I live in Rome.
  I live in …

Speaking

1 Stand up and introduce yourself to the person next to you. Say where you are from.
   Hi, I'm Marc. I'm from Italy.
2 Move to another person in the class and say where you are from in a different way.
   Hello, I'm Marc. I come from Italy, from Turin.
3 Repeat with three more people from the class.

Writing a form

Reading

1 Izaura is on holiday in the US. Read the form. Is it …

a   a travel booking form?   b   a US immigration form?

Family name: **OLIVEIRA**	
First (Given) name: **IZAURA**	Date of birth (mo/day/yr) : **11 / 14 / 86**
Country of citizenship: **BRAZIL**	Sex (male or female) : **FEMALE**
Passport number: **CM 278193**	Airline and flight number: **AA 125**
Country where you live: **ENGLAND**	City where you boarded: **LONDON**
Address while in the United States (number and street): **16, HARTFIELD AVE**	
City and state: **ALBANY, NEW YORK**	

2 Complete the text with information from the form.

My name's (1) _____. My date of birth is (2) _____. My flight is from (3) _____ and the flight number is (4) _____. My address in the US is (5) _____.

Writing skills: using capital letters

1 Read the rules about capital letters in English.

Use capital letters …
* to fill in forms.
* at the beginning of a sentence.
* with the pronoun I.
* with postcodes and the US, the UK.

Start these words with a capital letter:
a   names (of people, buildings)
b   roads and streets
c   days of the week
d   months
e   nationalities and languages
f   cities and towns
g   titles of books, films and newspapers

2 Match the words in the box to the rules a–g.

April   *Global Elementary*   High St.   Nelson Mandela
Russian   Saturday   Tokyo

3 Add capital letters to the text.

my name is andrea hunziker. my date of birth is 16th july 1972. i'm married. my address is 3, station rd, nottingham, ng3 6ae, uk. my telephone number is 0115 9691862 and my email address is andreahun3@hotmail.com.

Language focus: personal information

Match the words 1–8 to the information a–h.

1	address	a	Hunziker
2	date of birth	b	Andrea
3	email address	c	16.07.1972
4	first name	d	married
5	marital status	e	3, Station Rd, Nottingham
6	postcode	f	0115 9691862
7	surname	g	andreahun3@hotmail.com
8	telephone number	h	NG3 6AE

Preparing to write

Work in pairs. Ask and answer questions using the personal information words in the Language focus section. Use the useful phrases to help you.

A: *What's your address?*
B: *My address is ….*

Personal information

* What's your surname / first name / date of birth etc?
* I'm married / single / divorced / widowed.
* My surname / date of birth / postcode etc. is …

Writing

Complete the form with information about you and your partner.

	You	Your partner
Surname		
First name		
Date of birth		
Marital status		
Address		
Postcode		
Telephone number		
Email address		

Global review

Grammar

1 Write *a* or *an*.

1 ___ airport   2 ___ email   3 ___ hospital   4 ___ key

2 Write the plural forms of the nouns.

1 an address _____   3 a bus _____
2 a family _____   4 a name _____

3 Complete the conversation with the words in the box.

am	are	her	is	isn't	my	our	your

A: Good morning. (1) _____ you Mr Chen?
B: No, I (2) _____ Longfei Jin and this is (3) _____ daughter Xing Yan.
A: Welcome to the Clifton Hotel, Mr Jin. (4) _____ room is number 23. Here is the key.
B: Thank you. And Xing Yan? (5) _____ she in Room 24?
A: No, she (6) _____. She's in room 25. This is (7) _____ key.
B: Thank you. Here are (8) _____ passports.
A: Thank you very much. Enjoy your stay.

Vocabulary

1 Write the answers as words.

five + seven = twelve

1 nine + six = _____
2 thirteen + fourteen = _____
3 eleven + thirty-seven = _____
4 thirty-two + nineteen = _____
5 sixty-three + thirty-six = _____

2 Complete the sentences about the sentence below.

For many people in America and Western Europe, thirteen is an unlucky number.

Western is the seventh word in the sentence.

1 *Many* is _____ word in the sentence.
2 *Thirteen* is _____ word in the sentence.
3 *For* is _____ word in the sentence.
4 *America* is _____ word in the sentence.
5 *People* is _____ word in the sentence.

Speaking

1 Work in pairs. A: You are a guest at a hotel. B: You are the hotel receptionist. Ask the guest their name, address, phone number, email and car number plate. Tell the guest their room number. Then swap roles and repeat.

2 Work with a partner. A: say a letter. B: say an English word starting with the letter and spell it. Swap roles and repeat. Continue with more letters.

Study skills

Classroom language

1 Translate the classroom instructions into your language. Use a dictionary if necessary.

* Listen.
* Repeat.
* Write.
* Read.
* Open/close your book.
* Work in pairs.
* Ask your partner.
* Complete the sentences.
* Put the words in the correct order.
* Match the words to the pictures.
* Circle the correct answer.

2 Follow the instructions.

1 Put the words in the correct order.
   yellow plates number are
2 Match the numbers to the words.
   1   three
   2   one
   3   two
3 Underline the correct answer.
   two + two = *four / eight / twelve*
4 Complete the question.
   What's your phone _____ ?

3 Match the questions 1–4 to the answers a–d.

1 How do you spell *eight*?
2 What does *eight* mean?
3 How do you pronounce this word?
4 How do you say *acht* in English?

a It means the number after seven.
b E-I-G-H-T
c It's *eight* in English.
d /eɪt/

4 Work with a partner. Ask questions about the words in the box. Then ask about other words from the unit. Use the questions in exercise 3.

address	car	golf	hotel	juice	key	lucky
name	number	sandwich	telephone	thirteen		

What does address mean?

Where & When

Part 3

Listening

Telling the time

Vocabulary

Daily routine

Reading & Listening

The cross-border commuter

Grammar

Present simple (3rd person)

Pronunciation

/s/ /z/ /ɪz/

Speaking

A typical day

Listening

1 🔘 **1.42** Listen and repeat the times.

2 🔘 **1.43–1.45** Listen to three conversations and tick (✔) the times you hear.

3 Listen again. Match the conversations 1–3 to the subjects a–d. There is one subject you do not need.

a The time a train goes
b The time a party starts
c The time of a business meeting
d The time a film is on

4 Write down three times. Dictate them to a partner.

Vocabulary

1 Complete the table with the words in the box.

> a coffee   dinner   home   ~~home~~
> to the gym

go	to work / university	to a party	_home_	_____	to bed
have	breakfast	lunch	_____	a meeting	_____
get	up	to work	_____		

2 Put the phrases from exercise 1 in order to make a typical day for you. Then compare with a partner.

I get up, I have breakfast, I go to work …

Reading and Listening

1 🔘 **1.46** Read *The cross-border commuter*. Then listen and complete the table for Laura's Spanish day.

The cross-border commuter

Laura Clunie is English. She lives in London, and she works for an international company. Laura works three days a week in London, but she works in Barcelona on Thursdays and Fridays. Laura is a new Euro commuter – a person who lives in one European country and works in a different European country. Her daily life is different in the two countries.

Laura's British day	get up	7.00am
	have lunch	12.30pm
	have dinner	6.30pm
	go to bed	11.00pm
Laura's Spanish day	get up	8
	have lunch	2
	have dinner	9
	go to bed	12
Your _____ day	get up	_____
	have lunch	_____
	have dinner	_____
	go to bed	_____

2 What about you? Complete the table in exercise 1. Then compare your daily routine with a partner.

Studies say there will be more than 1.5 million Euro commuters by 2020.

The most popular Euro commutes are Paris – London and Barcelona – London.

Grammar

*I normally **have** lunch at about 12.30.*
*Laura **gets up** at 8.00 for work.*
*She **finishes** work at 7.30.*

- use the present simple to talk about routines
- for *he / she / it* add *s* or *es* to the verb

1 Read the two texts about Laura and underline the verbs. What's the difference between the verbs in text A and text B?

Text A
When I'm in London, I get up at 7.00 for work. I normally have lunch at about 12.30 or 1.00. I finish work at 5.30 and have dinner at 6.30. I normally go to bed about 10.30 or 11.00.

Text B
When she's in Barcelona, Laura gets up at 8.00 for work. She normally has lunch at about 2.00. She finishes work at 7.30 and has dinner at 9.00. She normally goes to bed about midnight.

Useful language

- 12.00pm = noon   • 12.00am = midnight

2 Write a similar text about your teacher. Don't ask questions, guess.

My teacher gets up at ...

3 Listen to your teacher talk about a typical day. Check your texts.

G **Grammar focus –** explanation & more practice of the present simple on page 138

Pronunciation

1 🔊 **1.47** Listen and repeat the sounds and words.

/s/	/z/	/ɪz/
gets	has	finishes
books	pens	buses

2 🔊 **1.48** Listen and write the words in the correct column.

airports	clocks	exercises	keys
phones	starts	watches	

3 🔊 **1.49** Try to say the phrases quickly. Then listen and repeat.

Clocks and watches.
These watches are Swiss watches.
Breakfasts, lunches and dinners.
She starts and finishes early.

Speaking

1 Choose four of the words below and make sentences about what times you do these things.

I normally get up at 7.00.

bed	breakfast	coffee	dinner
get up	gym	home	lunch	work

2 Work in groups of three. Compare your sentences with the other students in the group.

A: *I normally get up at 7.00.*
B: *Me too.*
C: *7.00? That's really early. I get up at 9.30.*

Where & When

Vocabulary and Listening

1 Read the text about time. Then complete the chart with the words from the text in bold. Do you agree with the text?

Seconds are short. **Minutes** are long.

Hours are short. **Days** are long.

Weeks are short. **Months** are long.

Years are short. **Decades** are long.

Life is short.

60 seconds	= 1 _____	
60 minutes	= 1 _____	
24 _____	= 1 _____	
7 _____	= 1 _____	
4 _____	= 1 _____	
12 _____	= 1 _____	
10 _____	= 1 _____	

2 Put the words in the box into two groups (months and days). Then put them in order in the table.

April	August	December	February
Friday	January	July	June	March
May	Monday	November	October
Saturday	Sunday	September	
Thursday	Tuesday	Wednesday	

Months	Days
January	

3 🔊 1.50 Listen and check your answers. Underline the stressed syllable.

> **Language note:** to say the date in English, use ordinal numbers.
> 1 January = *1ˢᵗ January*

4 🔊 1.51 Listen and circle the correct alternative.

1	13th July	13th June
2	12th August	20th August
3	21st May	31st May
4	2nd October	22nd October
5	3rd September	30th September
6	22nd March	2nd March

5 Work in pairs. A: turn to page 126. B: turn to page 128. Dictate some dates to your partner.

Reading and listening

1 Quickly read *When is New Year's Day?* on page 25. Tick (✔) the parts of the world the text mentions.

Western countries
Latin American countries
South Asia
Islamic countries

2 🔊 1.52 Read and listen to the text again. Which calendar …

1 has twelve months?
2 follows the sun and moon?
3 follows the moon?
4 follows the sun?
5 begins in October or November?
6 begins in January?

Grammar

> *The Islamic calendar* **doesn't use** *the sun.*
> *The Indian year* **doesn't begin** *in January.*

- form the negative with *don't / doesn't* + infinitive

1 Circle the correct option in each sentence.

1 The Gregorian calendar *don't use / doesn't use* the moon to measure time.
2 The Islamic calendar *don't use / doesn't use* the sun to measure time.
3 The Islamic and Indian calendars *don't start / doesn't start* on 1 January.

2 🔊 1.53 Complete the text with the correct form of the verb in brackets. Then listen and check your answers.

The Chinese calendar

The Chinese calendar _____ (*use*) the sun and the moon. It is different because it _____ (*not count*) years infinitely. On a Chinese calendar the years _____ (*have*) names: the Year of the Rat, Year of the Pig, etc and the cycle _____ (*repeat*) every 12 years. The Chinese New Year _____ (*not start*) on 1 January, it _____ (*start*) between January and February.

3 Complete these sentences so they are true for you.

I don't go to work on Sundays.
I don't … on Sundays.
I don't … in August.
I don't … in December.
We don't have English class …
I don't …
My teacher doesn't …

Ⓖ **Grammar focus** – explanation & more practice of the present simple on page 138

Writing

1 Read the text about favourite days below.

> My favourite day is Thursday because I don't work and I have lunch with my friends.
>
> My least favourite day is Monday because I start work very early.

2 Write about your favourite and least favourite days. Use *because* to explain your reasons.

My favourite day is … because …
My least favourite day is … because …

When is
NEW YEAR'S DAY?
Calendars from around the world

The Gregorian calendar (used by most Western countries) has 12 months and 365.242184 days. A year is the time it takes the earth to go around the sun. On a Gregorian calendar the New Year begins on 1 January.

The Islamic calendar also has 12 months, but it doesn't use the sun. It uses the moon. The New Year in an Islamic calendar begins in the month of Muharram – usually between November and February on a Gregorian calendar.

The Indian calendar also has 12 months. It uses the sun and the moon. But in the Indian calendar, the New Year doesn't begin in January. It begins in the holiday of Diwali. This is a very important festival in South Asia. Diwali is usually in October or November on a Gregorian calendar.

Function globally asking and telling the time

a b c d

Warm up

Work in pairs. Describe the pictures.

Useful language

• at night	• buses
• busy	• in the city
• in the country	• in the daytime
• modern	• new
• old	• people

Useful phrases

- This photo is of a …
- In this photo the bus station is …
- I think this bus station is in …

Listening

1 1.54–1.56 Listen to three conversations. Match each one to a destination in the box. There is one destination you do not need.

Mexico City	Ottawa	the airport	the city centre

2 Listen again and circle the time you hear.

1 The bus is at *5.50 / 5.15*.
2 The bus is at *2.15 / 2.50*.
3 The time is now *10.30 / 10.13*.

Language focus: asking and telling the time

1 1.57 Put the words in the correct order to make two ways of asking the time. Then listen and check.

1 time what is the?
2 what it time is?

2 Look at the diagram of how to tell the time in English. How do you say these times?

6.45 *six forty-five / a quarter to seven*
7.15
8.30
10.10
10.50
9.35

o'clock
five to — five past
ten to — ten past
a quarter to — a quarter past
twenty to — twenty past
twenty-five to — twenty-five past
half past

Speaking

Work with a partner. Choose **one** of the tasks below.

A Work in pairs. Write five times on a piece of paper. A: ask B the time. B: tell A the first time on your list. Then swap roles and repeat. Continue with all the times.

B Choose one of the pictures of bus stations. Prepare a conversation. Practise and present your conversation to another group.

Useful language

- Excuse me …
- What time is the bus for …
- When is the bus for …
- When is the next bus to …?
- What's the time?

Global English

Three circles of Global English
by David Crystal

When the Anglo-Saxons arrived in Britain, in the fifth century, speaking the original English there were just a few hundred of them. Today, the English-speaking population of the world is more than two billion …

Glossary

billion (*number*) – 1,000,000,000

million (*number*) - 1,000,000

An inner circle
Over 400 million native speakers in countries including Britain, the USA, Canada, Australia, New Zealand and South Africa.

An outer circle
At least 600 million people have learned English in countries that have a special relationship with Britain or the USA. For example Nigeria, the Philippines, India and more than 50 other countries.

An expanding circle
More than 1000 million non-native speakers in other countries: Europe, Latin America, Japan, Russia and China.

1 native speaker : 4 non-native speakers
For every native speaker of English today, there are about four non-native speakers: 400 million native speakers but over 1,600 million non-native speakers.

Warm up

1 Look at the title and list of country names. What are the missing letters?

Countries with E... as the official lan...
Cana...
Ind...
Irel...
Jamai...
Ken...
Pakis...
Singa...
Zimbab...

2 Can you think of any other countries for this list?

Reading

Read the text and match the numbers to the words.

1 1000 million (1,000,000,000)
2 400 million (400,000,000)
3 a few hundred (100s)
4 600 million (600,000,000)
5 2 billion (2,000,000,000)

a English native speakers today
b Non-native speakers of English
c Speakers from other countries that have a relationship with Britain or the US
d The Anglo-Saxons who arrived in England
e English-speaking population today

Language focus

What do the phrases mean? Choose the correct meaning. Use a dictionary to help you.

1 **more than** 400 million   < 400 million
   > 400 million

2 **over** 600 million   < 600 million
   > 600 million

3 **just** a few hundred   only a few hundred
   > a few hundred

4 **about** two billion   two billion (+ or −)
   < two billion

Speaking

Work in pairs and discuss the questions.

• How many different languages do people speak in your country?
• Do people speak your language in other countries?

Writing describing a routine

Reading

1 Read about Fariha's routine. Why is she busy at the moment?

I have a new job in a hotel. I get up at six fifteen and have breakfast at seven o'clock I go to work at eight o'clock I go home at one o'clock and then I have lunch in the afternoon, I do the housework I make dinner at six o'clock we have dinner at seven thirty after that, I watch TV or read on Wednesdays, I go to my English class I go to bed about ten thirty at weekends, I do exercise and meet my friends I visit my family on Sundays

2 Complete the sentences.

1 Fariha gets up at _____.
2 At seven o'clock she _____.
3 She does the housework in _____.
4 She makes dinner at _____.
5 She goes to her English class _____.
6 She goes to bed _____.

Writing skills: using full stops and commas

We use a full stop at the end of a sentence. A full stop is called a *period* in the US.

We use commas to separate parts of the sentence. *in the morning, on Saturdays …*

1 Find four commas in Fariha's description.

2 Add twelve full stops to Fariha's description. Write capital letters to start new sentences.

3 Correct the punctuation in the text below and add capital letters.

Fariha has a new job, she works in a hotel, she gets up very early, she goes to work at eight o'clock, after that she has lunch, in the afternoon she watches TV, she goes to bed about eleven o'clock

Language focus: time expressions

1 Match phrases 1–4 to a–d.

1 after breakfast   a in the evening
2 after lunch   b then
3 after dinner   c in the afternoon
4 after that   d in the morning

2 Complete the texts about Wieslaw's routine with expressions in the box.

> After breakfast   and then   In the afternoon
> In the evening   On weekdays

(1) _____ I get up at about seven o'clock and have breakfast at about eight o'clock. (2) _____ I go to college. I have lunch at twelve thirty. (3) _____ I study in the library. I go home at five o'clock, (4) _____ I have dinner. (5) _____ I usually watch TV. I go to bed early, about ten o'clock.

> After dinner   after lunch   after that   In the morning
> On Saturdays

(6) _____ I get up late, at about eleven o'clock and (7) _____ I have breakfast. (8) _____ I do my homework or listen to music. I have lunch at about one o'clock and (9) _____ I play football. I have dinner at about eight o'clock. (10) _____ I normally meet friends and we go to a party.

Preparing to write

1 Make notes about your daily routine.

2 Work in pairs. Tell your partner about your daily routine. Use the useful phrases to help you.

> ### Time expressions
> • On Mondays / Saturdays / weekdays …
> • In the morning / afternoon / evening …
> • On Sunday mornings / Monday afternoons / Saturday evenings …
> • At the weekend …
> • After breakfast / lunch / dinner …
> • After that / Then …

Writing

Write about your daily routine. Use your notes and the useful phrases to help you.

Global review

Grammar

1 Put the words in the correct order to make questions.

1 you where from are?
2 he old is how?
3 is capital the Japan what of?
4 English when class your is?
5 here you why are?

2 Complete the text about Martin's day using the correct form of the verbs in brackets.

Martin normally (1) _____ (*get*) up at about 7.00 and (2) _____ (*go*) to work at 8.30. He (3) _____ (*not have*) a big lunch. He (4) _____ (*finish*) work at 5.00 and (5) _____ (*have*) dinner at 7.00.

Vocabulary

1 Correct one word in each group.

1 Italian American Turkian Mexican
2 Polish Swedish Russish Scottish
3 Chinese Hollandese Vietnamese Japanese
4 Thai French Czech Germanch

2 Write the opposite adjectives.

1 a noisy place, a q_____ place
2 a big town, a s_____ town
3 an old city, a m_____ city

3 Write the dates in full.

4/10   *the fourth of November*
1 1/1   _____
2 13/3   _____
3 20/7   _____
4 22/12   _____

Speaking and Writing

1 Write four sentences about your daily routine. One must be false. Work in small groups. Take it in turns to read out your sentences and try to guess which one is false.

2 Write down a new name, city and country for yourself. Work in small groups. Imagine you are at a party. Ask each other questions to find out your new identities.

Study skills

Working with other people

If you don't understand someone, say *Pardon?* or *Sorry?* You can also use other questions and phrases.
Can you speak more slowly, please?
Sorry, I don't understand.
Can you repeat that, please?

1 Work in pairs. A: talk about your town or country. B: use some of the phrases in the box above. Then swap roles and repeat.

2 Look up the verbs in the box in a dictionary. Then work in pairs and circle the correct answers.

check   communicate   correct   explain

1 Who explains the meaning of words in class?
the teacher / the students / the teacher or the students
2 Who corrects mistakes in class?
the teacher / the students / the teacher or the students
3 Who checks homework?
the teacher / the students / the teacher or the students
4 Who communicates in class?
the teacher / the students / the teacher or the students

3 In class you can help each other in different ways. Look at the list and tick (✔) the things you do. Then work in small groups and compare your lists.

★ I explain words to my partner.
★ I ask my partner to explain words.
★ I correct my partner.
★ I ask my partner to correct me.
★ I explain how to do activities.
★ I explain grammar rules.
★ I check answers with my partner.
★ I use new language to communicate.

Family & Friends

Vocabulary

1 Complete the family tree with the words in the box.

aunt	grandfather	sister	son	wife

2 Work in pairs. Ask each other these questions.

How many … do you have?

- brothers
- sisters
- cousins
- uncles
- aunts
- children
- grandchildren

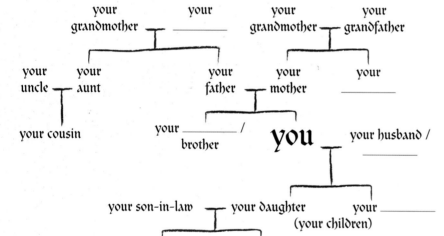

Reading

1 You are going to read about some famous families in English literature. Before you read, check you understand these words.

dead	enemy	jealous
land	power	revenge

2 🔊 1.58 Read and listen to *Shakespeare's tragic families* on page 31. Are these statements true (T) or false (F)?

1 King Lear has two daughters.
2 Hamlet is from Denmark.
3 Hamlet's mother isn't married.
4 Lady Macbeth and Macbeth are brother and sister.
5 Juliet's last name is Capulet.
6 Iago is married to Desdemona.

3 Read the texts again and match the families to the diagrams of the family trees below.

1 *Hamlet*
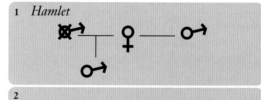

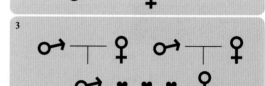

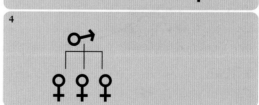

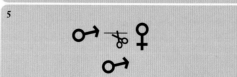

4 Do you know any of these stories?

Grammar

> *King Lear's daughters*
> *Hamlet's mother*
> *Romeo's girlfriend*
> *Her parents' names are Lord and Lady*
> *Capulet*
>
> - use **'s** to show possession
> - if a word ends in **s**, add **'**

1 Look at the texts again. Find the answers to these questions.

Who is …

1 Cordelia's father?
2 Hamlet's uncle?
3 Macbeth's wife?
4 Romeo's girlfriend?
5 Desdemona's husband?

2 Complete the texts with possessive *'s*. There are four missing.

Julius Caesar
He is Dictator of Rome, but for how long? Are Caesar friends now his enemies? Calpurnia, Caesar wife, thinks they are. A story of power and revenge.

Antony and Cleopatra
Antony wife Fluvia is dead. He now lives in Egypt with the Queen Cleopatra. But Antony's rival Octavius wants him to return to Rome. A story of love and power.

3 Choose four members of your family and tell a partner their names.

my mother
My mother's name is Sandra.
my father
my brother / sister
my children
my grandparents
my grandchildren

G **Grammar focus** – explanation & more practice of possessive *'s* on page 140

Shakespeare's
tragic families

King Lear: King Lear loves his three daughters: Cordelia, Regan and Goneril. But do the daughters love their father? A story of land, money and power.

Hamlet: In Denmark, Prince Hamlet's father is dead, and his mother Gertrude is now married to Claudius – Hamlet's uncle. A story of a son's love and revenge.

Macbeth: A story of Macbeth and his wife, Lady Macbeth. Lady Macbeth wants power, and she wants her husband to be the king. A story of revenge and power.

Romeo and Juliet: Romeo is the son of Lord and Lady Montague. Juliet is the daughter of Lord and Lady Capulet. Romeo and Juliet are boyfriend and girlfriend. But their families are enemies. A love story.

Othello: Iago is Othello's friend, or is he? He makes trouble for Othello and his wife Desdemona. A story of a jealous husband.

Writing

1 Write a short text (two to three sentences) about your family. Use the useful phrases to help you.

Useful phrases

- My family is from …
- My mother's / father's name is …
- My parents are from …
- I have … brothers / sisters / children.

2 Work in pairs. Exchange texts and write one question about your partner's family.

What are your children's names?
Where are your grandparents from?

3 Give your paper back to your partner. Rewrite your text including the answer to the question.

Family & Friends

Vocabulary

1 🔘 **1.59** Write the missing vowels to complete the colours. Listen and check your answers. Then repeat the colours.

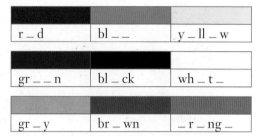

r _ d	bl _ _	y _ ll _ w
gr _ _ n	bl _ ck	wh _ t _
gr _ y	br _ wn	_ r _ ng _

2 🔘 **1.60** Look at the pictures of tartans and listen to the descriptions of their colours. Number the pictures in the order you hear them.

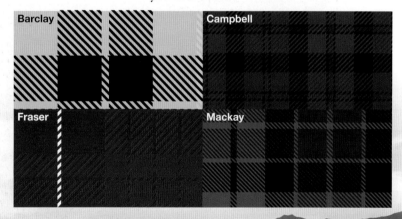

Barclay

Campbell

Fraser

Mackay

Reading and Listening

1 🔘 **1.61** Read and listen to *Clans* on page 33 and tick (✔) the correct sentences.

1 A clan is a type of family group.
2 All Scottish people are part of a clan.
3 Tartan is a special material for kilts.
4 Scottish people wear kilts on special occasions.

2 🔘 **1.62–1.63** Listen to two Scottish people talk about clans. Circle the correct answers in the table.

Name	Hilary Thomson	Gordon Liddle
From?	Edinburgh Glasgow Dundee	Edinburgh Glasgow Dundee
Lives in?	Edinburgh Madrid London	Edinburgh Glasgow Dundee
Has a family clan?	Yes No	Yes No
Wears a kilt?	Yes No	Yes No
Thinks clans are important?	Yes No	Yes No

3 Do you know any Scottish people? Tell a partner.

Grammar

> *Do* you *live* in Scotland?
> Yes, I *do*. No, I *don't*.
> *Does* he *have* a family clan?
> Yes, he *does*. No, he *doesn't*.

- use *do* with *I*, *you*, *we* and *they*
- use *does* with *he*, *she* and *it*

1 Complete the sentences with *do* / *don't* / *does* / *doesn't*.

A: _____ you live in Edinburgh now?
B: No, I _____. I live in Madrid in Spain.
A: _____ you have a family clan?
B: Yes, we _____. We're part of the Campbell clan.

A: _____ he live in Scotland?
B: No, he _____. He lives in England.
A: _____ he wear a kilt?
B: Yes, he _____.
A: _____ he think clans are important for Scottish people?
B: No, he _____.

2 🔊 **1.64** Put the words in the correct order to make questions. Then listen and check your answers.

1 big / family / do / you / a / have?
2 children / have / you / do?
3 with your parents / you / do / live?
4 in a different country / you / do / have family?
5 at the weekend / do / have lunch / you / with your family?
6 in your family / work / do / with someone / you?

3 Work in pairs. Ask each other the questions in exercise 2.

Ⓖ **Grammar focus** – explanation & more practice of questions on page 140

The Campbell crest

Clans

Clan is a Gaelic word. It means family. A clan is a type of historical family group. A lot of people in Scotland are part of a clan. Scottish clans have a material with a special pattern – tartan. Many Scottish people wear a kilt in their clan tartan on special occasions such as weddings.

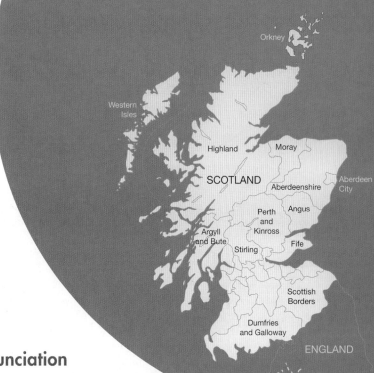

Orkney

Western Isles

Highland   Moray

SCOTLAND   Aberdeenshire   Aberdeen City

Perth and Kinross   Angus

Argyll and Bute   Stirling   Fife

Scottish Borders

Dumfries and Galloway

ENGLAND

Pronunciation

1 🔊 **1.65** Listen to the intonation in this question from Grammar exercise 2.

Do you have a big family?

2 Listen again and repeat the questions in Grammar exercise 2.

Speaking

Walk around the class. Ask questions to complete the task.

Find someone who ...
- has a big family.
- has children.
- lives with their parents.
- has family in a different country.
- has lunch with their family at the weekend.
- works with someone in their family.

Speaking

1 Write the names of three friends.

2 Work in pairs. Ask questions about your partner's friends. Use ideas from the box below.

Where's Sven from?

From?
Married?
Children?
Work / Study together?

Reading

1 You are going to read a text about friends and meeting places. Check you understand the words in bold in the box.

at **home**	at the **mall**	at the **market**
at the **park**	in the **square**	

Language note: *a mall* is American English. In British English it is usually called *a shopping centre*.

2 Read *Meeting places around the world*. Which places in the box in exercise 1 go with each paragraph? There is one place you do not need.

Language note: we use the verbs *love*, *like*, *don't like* and *hate* + noun to say how much we find things enjoyable.

love
like
don't like
hate

*I **love** parties.*
*I **hate** early mornings.*

Meeting places around the world

Abu Dhabi, United Arab Emirates

In my country, young women meet up at home. My friend Shamsa lives in a big house and we all go there and have a little party. (1) _____. We have something to eat and we talk about our friends, our parents, fashion – everything! We have a great time.

Hanoi, Vietnam

I normally see my friends at the *Hoàn Kiêm* Lake. It's very beautiful. (2) _____. We go for a walk and talk a lot.

Dallas, US

My friends and I go to the mall. Sometimes we see a film or go shopping, but normally we just walk round and talk. The guys sometimes play video games (3) _____! I prefer window shopping.

Florence, Italy

All our friends live in the same part of town. We usually go to the main square – *la Piazza del Signoria* and go for a walk and talk. We meet in the early evening (4) _____.

3 Read the text again. Complete the gaps in the text with the phrases below.

a but I hate computers

b because we like a walk before dinner

c I don't like busy places – I prefer to be outdoors

d We all love parties

4 Where do you meet your friends? Tell a partner.

Vocabulary

1 Write the verb from the text that goes with each group of expressions.

1	_meet_	up in the evening near work
2	_____	in a big house in the same part of town about five minutes from here
3	_____	about our friends / family a lot
4	_____	for a walk shopping to a restaurant
5	_____	a film my friends
6	_____	video games football

2 Write four sentences to describe what you do with your friends when you meet up. Use the expressions in exercise 1.

I meet up with my friends in the evening.

We play football.

Grammar

Where do you and your friends meet?

- use a *Wh-* question word + the auxiliary *do / does* to make questions in the present simple

1 Put the words in the correct order to make questions.

live where you do?

Where do you live?

1 see where you do friends your?

2 you your meet when friends do?

3 meet why you do there?

4 do do what you?

2 Look at the questions in exercise 1. Change the subject to *he*.

Where do you live?

Where does he live?

3 Work in pairs. Read about another meeting place. Then answer the questions in exercise 2.

Limerick, Ireland

I normally meet some old school friends at a local pub. We meet on a Friday evening. We go there because it's close to work. We sit and talk and we sometimes watch the football.

G **Grammar focus** – explanation & more practice of *Wh-* questions on page 140

Speaking

Work in pairs. Ask each other the questions in Grammar exercise 1. Then work with a new partner. Tell them what you found out.

Noriko meets her friends in the park.

Family & Friends

Part 4

Vocabulary
Adjectives to describe characteristics

Reading & Listening
Man's best friend?

Grammar
Object pronouns

Pronunciation
Emphasising

Vocabulary

1 Match the adjectives to their opposites. Which adjectives are positive (+) and which are negative (-)?

1	intelligent	a	awful
2	clean	b	ugly
3	friendly	c	stupid
4	nice	d	dirty
5	beautiful	e	unfriendly

> **Language note:** the adjective comes **before** the noun in English.
> *It is an **intelligent** animal.*

2 Choose three of the animals below. How would you describe these animals? Use the words in exercise 1.

They're beautiful.

It's an intelligent animal.

Reading and Listening

1 💿 **1.66** Read and listen to *Man's best friend?* on page 37 and find three things dogs are used for.

2 💿 **1.67** Listen to six people talking about dogs. Circle the correct option.

Speaker 1 *likes / dislikes* dogs.
Speaker 2 *likes / dislikes* dogs.
Speaker 3 *likes / dislikes* dogs.
Speaker 4 *likes / dislikes* dogs.
Speaker 5 *likes / dislikes* dogs.
Speaker 6 *likes / dislikes* dogs.

3 Listen again. Answer the questions.

1 What does the speaker think of dogs?
2 How old is Jupiter?
3 What animals does speaker 3 **not** like?
4 What does the speaker say about Rufus?
5 What is the problem with Princess?
6 Speaker 6 doesn't have a dog. Why?

4 Do you agree that dogs are *man's best friend*? Why?

> ### Extend your vocabulary – *really*
>
> *really* = very
> It is very common in spoken English.
> This dog is really intelligent. = This dog is very intelligent.
> He really likes dogs. = He likes dogs very much.
> Give examples of …
> 1 a really ugly city.
> 2 a person you really like.
> 3 a really intelligent animal.
> 4 a really beautiful place.

dolphins   a horse   a dog

a cat   camels   a rat

Grammar

> *Dogs? I really hate **them**.*
> *She doesn't like **me** very much.*
>
> - use *me*, *you*, *him*, *her* etc. after the verb in statements
> - the pronouns *it* and *you* have the same form for subject and object

1 Circle the correct option. Then check your answers in the audioscript on page 153.

1 I really hate *they / them*. *They / Them* are awful animals.
2 We have a dog, Jupiter. *He / Him* is 16 years old, he's intelligent, friendly and we love *him / he*.
3 *I / Me* like dogs.
4 Personally, I don't like *he / him* very much.
5 *I / Me* love my dog. *She / Her* name is Princess.
6 *We / Us* would like a dog. *We / Us* love *they / them*.

2 Replace the underlined word with a subject or object pronoun.

Cats are very popular animals for the home. People like <u>cats</u> because <u>cats</u> are clean. <u>Cats</u> don't need to go for a walk every day. Some people hate cats. <u>Cats</u> have a reputation as unfriendly animals.

People say that a dog is a man's best friend and I agree. My dog Jack is definitely my best friend. My wife and I have two small children and <u>Jack</u> is really good with <u>the children</u>. <u>My wife and the children and I</u> all love <u>Jack</u>.

(G) Grammar focus – explanation & more practice of object pronouns on page 140

Pronunciation

1 🔊 1.68 Listen and repeat the phrases.
1 Do you like dogs? Dogs? I hate them.
2 Do you like cats? Cats? I love them.

2 Make similar exchanges. Use the verbs and nouns in the box for ideas.

| hate | like | love |
| football | school | shopping |

Man's best friend ?

The relationship between dogs and humans is more than 12,000 years old.

People use dogs for defence, for carrying things, for transport and even for food.

In many parts of the world, people use dogs as companions and pets in the home. The care of dogs in the United States and Britain is a multi-billion dollar business.

War dogs from Ancient Rome

Sled dogs in North America

A sniffer dog at an international airport

A guide dog for the blind

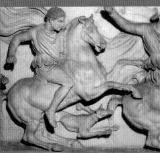

Famous dog lovers

Alexander the Great (356–323 BC), King of Macedonia
Dog's name: **Peritas**

Dwight D. Eisenhower (1890–1969), US President
Dog's name: **Heidi**

Pablo Picasso (1881–1973), Spanish artist
Dog's name: **Kasbec**

Function globally showing interest

Warm up

1 Choose **one** of the topics from the box. Think of two or three things you can say about this topic.

| a friend   a member of your family   you   your town |

2 Work in pairs. A: tell B about your topic. Try to talk for 30 seconds. B: listen to A. Then swap roles and repeat.

Listening

1 🔊 **1.69–1.72** Listen to four conversations. Match each one to a picture.

2 Listen again. Choose the correct answer.

1 The man is from …
   a Hungary.   b Romania.   c Scotland.
2 Michael's birthday is in …
   a January.   b June.   c July.
3 Alan lives …
   a with the woman.   b with his parents.
   c with his wife.
4 At 7.00am, the man …
   a starts work.   b finishes work.   c goes to work.

Language focus: showing interest

Language note: repeating words and asking questions shows interest in what the other person is saying.

Complete the responses from the listening. Repeat a word and add a question in the box.

| How old is he?   What part of Romania? |
| Why do you start so early?   When's his birthday? |

1 I'm from Romania.
   Romania ? _____ ?
2 He's two years old.
   _____ ? _____ ?
3 Well, he still lives with his parents.
   _____ ? _____ ?
4 Seven o'clock in the morning.
   _____ ? _____ ?

Speaking

Work in pairs. A: tell B about a topic from Warm up exercise 1. Try to talk for 30 seconds. B: listen to A. Use the techniques in the language focus to show interest. Then swap roles and repeat.

Global voices

Warm up

1 Complete the sentences about families with your own ideas.

1. A big family has _____ or more people.
2. A small family has _____ people.
3. A very small family has _____ people.
4. A typical family in my country has _____ people.

2 Work in pairs and compare your answers.

Listening

Nicole, Switzerland   Carmen, Spain   Martin, Czech Republic

Dot, Scotland   Bea, England   Ena, Bosnia

1 🎧 1.73–1.78 Listen to six people talking about their families. Circle the correct option.

1. Nicole, Switzerland
   big family / small family / doesn't say
2. Carmen, Spain
   big family / small family / doesn't say
3. Martin, Czech Republic
   big family / small family / doesn't say
4. Dot, Scotland
   big family / small family / doesn't say
5. Bea, England
   big family / small family / doesn't say
6. Ena, Bosnia
   big family / small family / doesn't say

2 Listen again and complete the sentences.

1. Nicole has _____ brother/brothers.
2. There are _____ people in Carmen's family.
3. Martin's mother has _____ sister/sisters.
4. Dot has _____ brother/brothers.
5. Bea has _____ sister/sisters.
6. Ena has _____ brother/brothers.

Language focus: *a lot of, lots of*

1 Read the language note. Then add *a lot of* or *lots of* in the appropriate places in the sentences below.

> **Language note:** *a lot of/lots of* = a large number
> Use *a lot of/lots of* with plural nouns and uncountable nouns.
> *I have a lot of books.*
> *There's a lot of food.*
> (See unit 4 for more on uncountable nouns.)

1. My mother has two sisters, so I have cousins.
2. My parents don't have brothers and sisters. I have only one cousin.
3. My friends live with their parents.
4. Are people in your family from Russia?
5. I have a small family. I don't have brothers or sisters, only one brother.

Speaking

Work in groups. Ask questions to find out if the sentences below are true. If they are false change them so they are true.

- Everybody in this group has a brother or sister.
- Everybody in this group has cousins.
- Two people in this group are parents.
- Only one person in the group has a grandson or granddaughter.
- Everybody in this group has a family member in a different country.

Useful phrases

- Do you have …   any brothers or sisters?
                   a brother in a different country?
                   any children?

Writing a personal description

Reading

1 Read Patricia's letter to her teacher. Does she have a big family?

Dear Oliver

My name Patricia. Im from Madrid in Spain. I work for a bank. I speak Spanish and a little English. I like travelling and shopping.

My husband name is Carlos. He an engineer. He likes sports and films. We have a daughter called Claudia. She ten years old and she studies English at the English Institute too. She likes skiing and playing tennis. I think she speaks English very well.

My parents are retired. I have two brothers. My first brother called Felipe. He a lawyer and he married to Alejandra. They have two daughters called Isabel and Maria Eugenia. My second brother name is Fernando. He a doctor, and he works in a hospital. He isnt married.

Thank you for your teaching. I'm very happy to be in your class.

Best wishes

Patricia

2 Are these sentences true (T) or false (F)?

1 Patricia is married.
2 Claudia likes sports.
3 Alejandra is Felipe's mother.
4 Patricia likes her English class.

Language focus: names

1 Complete the sentences about Patricia.

1 My name's _____.
2 My husband's name is _____.
3 My husband's called _____.
4 We have a daughter called _____.

2 Write sentences including the words below.

1 My / son / called Antonio. _____.
2 My / sister / name / Rosa. _____.
3 I / have / son /called / Xavier. _____.
4 My / name / Maria. _____.

Writing skills: apostrophes

Patricia wrote *My name Patricia* ✘
The correct sentence is *My name's Patricia* ✔

1 Read the rules about apostrophes in English.

Use apostrophes …
a with singular nouns to show possession.
  my husband's name, Felipe's daughters
b with plural nouns to show possession.
  my brothers' daughters, my parents' names
c with verb contractions.
  I'm, you're, she's, it's, Patricia's
d with contractions of *not*.
  we aren't, he isn't, they don't, he doesn't

2 Find ten more places in Patricia's letter where she does not use apostrophes.

3 Which of the examples are …

1 possessives?
2 contractions of *is or am*?

4 Add ten apostrophes to the text about Maria Jose.

My names Maria Jose and Im from Almeria. My husbands name is Marco. He isnt Spanish. Hes from Italy. My fathers an engineer and my mother doesnt work. My sisters names are Emilia and Raul. Theyre married and their husbands names are Jose and Rafael.

Preparing to write

Work in pairs. Draw your family tree and tell your partner about your family. Use the useful phrases to help you.

Describing your family

- I have one brother and two sisters.
- His name is … / He's called …
- I have a son called …
- He's retired / married / single / divorced.
- She's ten (years old).

Writing

1 Write a letter to your teacher. Write about yourself and your family.

2 Work in pairs. Exchange letters with your partner. Correct any mistakes.

Global review

Grammar

1 Correct one word in each sentence.

1 My sister name is Dominica.
2 We like our cat but she doesn't like we.
3 My grandparent's names are Lucy and Frederick.
4 I hate parties but my friends love they.
5 I love my brother but I don't see her very often.

2 Complete the questions.

1 Do _____?
  Yes, I really like video games.
2 Where _____?
  I live near the park.
3 Where _____?
  Sven works in New York.
4 When _____?
  Mario meets his friends in the evening.
5 What _____?
  Anna and Magda go shopping at the weekend.

Vocabulary

Complete the sentences.

1 Your uncle's son is your _____.
2 The opposite of *beautiful* is _____.
3 Your father's father is your _____.
4 Yellow and red make _____.
5 Black and white make _____.
6 Your daughter's children are your _____.
7 The opposite of *nice* is _____.
8 The opposite of *clean* is _____.
9 Your mother's sister is your _____.
10 Blue and yellow make _____.

Speaking

1 Work in pairs. Ask ten questions about your partner's family. Then tell the class about it.

2 Write five true sentences about your evenings using the words in the box.

| go | meet | play | see | talk about |

I talk about music with my friends. I don't play football.

3 Work in pairs. Read your sentences to your partner. Are any of their sentences the same as yours?

Study skills

Dictionary skills 1: using a learner's dictionary

1 Work in pairs. Answer the questions about using a dictionary. Then compare your answers.

1 What kind of dictionary do you have?
  a a bilingual dictionary
  b a monolingual learner's dictionary
  c an electronic / online dictionary
2 When do you use your dictionary?
  a at home
  b in class
  c at home and in class
3 Why do you use a dictionary?
  a to look up the meaning of English words
  b to translate words into English
  c to check the spelling of words
  d to check the pronunciation of words
  e to check how to use words

2 Look at the entry for *intelligent* from the *Macmillan Essential Dictionary* and answer the questions.

> intelligent ɪnˈtelɪdʒ(ə)nt (*adjective*)
> good at thinking, understanding and learning = CLEVER
> ≠ UNINTELLIGENT: *He was* **highly intelligent**, *but disliked studying.*

1 What is the meaning of *intelligent*?
2 What kind of word is it? (noun, adjective, verb etc)
3 How do you pronounce *intelligent*?
4 What is the opposite of *intelligent*?
5 Which word means the same as *intelligent*?
6 What is the example sentence for *intelligent*?

3 Read the sentences and look up the highlighted words in your dictionary. Which questions in exercise 2 can you answer for each word?

1 I'm always **busy** on Saturdays.
2 My **neighbour's** name is Katya.
3 Mr Moss is very **rude**.
4 In the evening I **chat** with friends.

Bed & Breakfast

Vocabulary

1 Match the phrases in the box to the pictures. Say the words.

> airport transfer   bar   cable television
> car park   guided tours   gym
> internet access   meeting room
> restaurant   swimming pool

2 Work in pairs. Choose one of the situations below. What are the two most important facilities for you?

- You are on holiday with two small children. You are at the hotel for three days and three nights.
- You are on a business trip. You are at the hotel for one night and you have an important meeting. You have a flight early the next morning.
- You are with your wife / husband. You are in the hotel for one night and then you are driving to a different city.

Reading

1 Look at the pictures and quickly read the texts on page 43. What is the best title?

1 Unusual places to spend the night
2 Expensive places to spend the night
3 Romantic places to spend the night

2 Choose the correct answer. Sometimes more than one answer is possible.

1 Where can you sleep for $120?
   a train   b jail   c tepee
2 Which hotel has a restaurant?
   a tepee   b train   c jail
3 Where can you go with a group?
   a jail   b tepee   c train
4 Where do you sleep in a building?
   a jail   b tepee   c train
5 Where can you sleep and study?
   a train   b tepee   c jail

3 🔊 **2.01** Read and listen to the texts again and complete the sentences with one or more words.

1 Trains or buses stop at a _____. (text 1)
2 The _____ is the part of the train where people eat. (text 1)
3 The American word for the shopping or business centre of a city is _____. (text 2)
4 If you want to know the _____ of something, you can ask 'How much is it?' (text 3)
5 A holiday that includes hotel, transport and food and extras is a _____ holiday. (text 3)

4 Complete the sentences with your own ideas. Then compare with a partner.

I think the most interesting place is …
I wouldn't like to stay at …

Grammar

> *The Guatemalan family eats **a lot of** fruit.*
> *They don't eat **much** processed food.*
> *The American family don't eat **many** vegetables.*
> *They eat **some** fruit.*

a lot of /
lots of   not much /
                                not many
                    some

- use *a lot of / lots of* and *some* with countable and uncountable nouns
- use *not much* with uncountable nouns
- use *not many* with countable nouns

1 Read the sentences and correct the mistakes.

1 The Guatemalan family eat lot of tomatoes.
2 The American family eat some of pizzas.
3 The American family don't eat much tomatoes.
4 The Guatemalan family eat some fruits.
5 The American family don't eat many of healthy food.

2 Complete the sentences so they are true for you.

- I don't eat much …
- I eat lots of …
- I drink some …
- I don't eat many …
- I drink lots of …

G Grammar focus – explanation & more practice of quantifiers on page 140

Writing

1 Choose **one** of the tasks below.

A Peter Menzel takes a photograph of your family and a week's food. What is in the photo? Write your answer.

In my photo, there is / are …
There is / are lots of …
There is / are some …

B You visit one of the families in the photos and they ask you what you would like for dinner. Plan a menu, based on what you see in the photos.

I would like … and … and some …

2 Work in pairs and swap texts. What do you have in common?

United States

Guatemala

Function globally making and responding to offers

Warm up

Work in pairs. A: you are invited to B's house for dinner. You arrive. B: you open the door. A is there. Read and continue the conversation.

A: Hello.
B: Hi. You're here. Come in.
A: Thanks. How are you?
B: I'm fine thanks. And you?

Listening

1 ⟳ 2.13–2.15 Listen to three conversations. Match each one to a situation.

- at a person's house
- in a company
- at a hotel

2 Listen again. Answer the questions.

Conversation 1: Does the woman smoke?
Conversation 2: Does the man have a coffee?
Conversation 3: What does the woman give?

Language focus: making and responding to offers

Making offers	*Would you like + a / an + noun?* Would you like a drink?
	Would you like + to + verb? Would you like to meet your colleagues?
Responding to offers	Yes, please. That would be great. No, thank you. Thank you very much, but I'm fine.

1 ⟳ 2.16 Read the information in the table. Then listen and write an offer with the word or phrase you hear.

A coffee
Would you like a coffee?

2 Work in pairs. Ask and answer the questions in exercise 1. Give different responses.

Speaking

Work in pairs. Choose **one** of the tasks below.

A Look at the audioscript on page 154 and choose one of the conversations. Change some of the information and then practise the conversation.

B Choose one of the situations from Listening exercise 1. Practise the conversation with the new expressions of making and responding to offers.

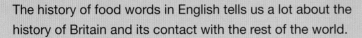

Global English

Delicious English

by David Crystal

The history of food words in English tells us a lot about the history of Britain and its contact with the rest of the world.

The oldest words, in Anglo-Saxon times, from the fifth century, were *bread*, *butter*, and *fish*, with *water*, *wine*,
5 and *beer* to wash them down. *Meat* described any food in those days.

In the 11th century, the French arrived in Britain, and there were interesting new dishes, such as *pheasant*, *oyster*, *biscuit*, and *pastry*. *Pork* and *veal* arrived for the upper-
10 class table. *Breakfast* is Anglo-Saxon, but *dinner* and *supper* are French.

By Shakespeare's time, in the 16th century, voyages around the world added more dishes to the menu. People started to eat *potatoes*, *anchovies*, *macaroni*, *curry* and
15 *yoghurt* and drink *coffee*, *tea* and *sherry*. And so, with *kippers* and *ice cream* in the 18th century, and *hamburgers* and *chips* in the 19th, we eventually arrive at where we are today, with *tacos* and *salsa*, *goulash* and *sushi*, *Coca-Cola*® and *Chardonnay*.

Glossary

Chardonnay (*noun*) – a type of white wine

eventually (*adverb*) – after some time

dishes (*noun*) – different kinds of food

kipper (*noun*) – smoked fish

pork (*noun*) – meat from a pig

sherry (*noun*) – a strong wine from Spain

such as – for example

veal (*noun*) – meat from a calf (a young cow)

voyage (noun) – a long journey

wash them down (*verb*) – drink something with food

Warm up

Where is it from? Match the food or drink to a country. Use your dictionary to help.

1	curry	a	Hungary
2	Coca-Cola®	b	India
3	goulash	c	Italy
4	pizza	d	Japan
5	paella	e	Mexico
6	sushi	f	Spain
7	tacos	g	the US

Reading

1 Read the text about food. When did people start to use these words in English?

biscuit	breakfast	chips	Coca-Cola®	coffee
curry	dinner	fish	hamburgers	ice cream
potatoes	supper	sushi	tacos	water

from the fifth century	
from the 11th century	
from the 16th century	
in the 18th & 19th centuries	
in the 21st century	

2 Choose the correct sentence, a or b, from each pair.

1 a All food words in English are from England.
  b English food words are from different countries at different times.
2 a Some names for meals are from French.
  b All the names for meals are from French.
3 a In Shakespeare's time new food and drink arrived.
  b In Shakespeare's time new food arrived.
4 a There are new words from recent times.
  b New words stopped in the 19th century.

Language focus

Look at the example: *Wine is a kind of drink.*

Write similar sentences to describe the words below, using the nouns/words in the box.

| drink | vegetable | dairy product | pasta |

1	tea …	4	butter …
2	macaroni …	5	Coca-Cola® …
3	potato …	6	yoghurt …

Speaking

Think of 3 foreign words for food or drink in your language and tell your partner.

Writing an email to a hotel

Reading

1 Read Shih-Chieh's email to a hotel and answer the questions.

1 What questions does he ask about the hotel?
2 What does he want the hotel to send?

> Dear Sir / Madam,
>
> I want to book a room at your hotel from April 7th to April 11th (four nights). I want a single room. I want a non-smoking room with a bath and shower. If possible, I want a balcony. I also want to have breakfast. Do you have a room available? What is the price?
>
> I have some other questions. Does the hotel have internet access? Is there a car park? What time do you serve breakfast?
>
> Please send me information about transport to the hotel from the airport.
>
> Yours faithfully,
>
> Shih-Chieh Liao

Language focus: making requests

1 Read about making requests in a formal letter or email.

When you say what you want, write *I would like …*, not ~~I want~~

I would like <u>to book a room</u>
I would like <u>a sea view</u>

To make a request, write *Could you please …?*
Could you please send me a map?

2 Complete these sentences with *I would like* or *Could you please*.

1 _____ to have dinner on the first night.
2 _____ send me information about the town?
3 If possible, _____ a quiet room.
4 _____ book me a taxi from the airport?

3 Make six changes to Shih-Chieh's email using *I would like* and *Could you please*.

Writing skills: starting and ending letters and emails

1 Look at the ways of starting and ending a letter or email.

a Dear Sir / Madam, … Yours faithfully,
b Hi Angela, … Love,
c Dear Ms Benko, … Yours sincerely,
d Dear Peter, … Best wishes,

2 Which of the expressions in exercise 1 do you use …

1 in a formal letter when you know the person's name?
2 in a formal letter when you don't know the person's name?
3 in an informal letter to a close friend?
4 in an informal letter, but not to a close friend?

Preparing to write

1 Complete the table about a hotel you would like to book.

Number of nights	
Arrival date	
Departure date	
Type of room	
Meals	
Special requests	
Questions	

2 Work in pairs. A: imagine you work in a hotel. B: phone the hotel to book a room. Use the useful phrases to help you. Then swap roles and repeat.

Booking a hotel

- I would like a single / double / twin room with a balcony / internet access / en suite facilities / a shower / a bath.
- If possible, I would like a smoking room / a quiet room / a sea view.
- Could you please send me information about transport / local restaurants / local entertainment / taxis from the airport?

Writing

Write an email to the hotel to book the room. Use your notes to help you.

Global review

Grammar

Circle the correct option.

1. There is *a / some / any* bar in the hotel.
2. There *is / are / aren't* any biscuits in the cupboard.
3. There is *any / a lot of / a* milk in the fridge.
4. We don't have *much / many / some* coffee.
5. Are there any *cheese / bananas / pizza* in the fridge?
6. I eat lots of *bread / biscuit / apple*.
7. There aren't *some / many / much* restaurants near here.
8. There *is / are / isn't* much milk in this coffee.
9. Is there *much / a / many* lamp in the room?
10. I don't eat *much / many / a* French fries.

Vocabulary

1 Put the words in the box into the table.

| armchair | bed | cooker | fridge | gym | shower |
| sofa | swimming pool | toilet | wardrobe | | |

bathroom	
bedroom	
kitchen	
hotel facilities	

2 Decide which word in each group is different. Why is it different?

milk   butter   cheese   meat

Meat is different because it isn't a kind of dairy product.

1. coffee   orange   juice   jam   tea
2. orange   biscuit   banana   apple
3. carrot   bean   potato   rice
4. apple juice   egg   bread   marmalade

Speaking

1 Work in pairs. A: you are a tourist. Ask your partner about places and facilities near the school. Then swap roles and repeat.

A: *Is there a restaurant near here?*

B: *Yes, there is. There's a Chinese restaurant. It's five minutes from here.*

2 Work in small groups. Tell your group about eating and drinking habits in your country, or a different country.

In China we eat a lot of rice. We don't eat much cheese ...

Study skills

Learning new words

1 Tick (✔) the sentences that are true for you. Then compare with a partner.

How do you learn new words in English?

- ★ I look them up in a dictionary and copy the entry.
- ★ I write new words in a vocabulary book.
- ★ I learn groups of words.
- ★ I write new words in a sentence.
- ★ I learn a number of new words every day.
- ★ other

2 Read about how one student uses vocabulary cards to learn new words.

I make cards and on one side I write a word and on the other side I draw a picture of the word, or write a sentence with a gap. I look at the pictures or sentences and try to remember the words. Then I turn over to check. It's a good way to learn new words.

| there | _____ are three rooms in my house. |

3 Make two vocabulary cards for words from this unit. Then work in small groups and show your pictures or sentences to people in your group. Can they guess the words on the other side?

4 Read about how a different student uses vocabulary cards.

I write the names of objects or sentences on cards. Then I put the cards on the objects in my house. Every time I see the cards, it helps me learn the words.

5 Work in pairs and decide what cards you can make for these rooms.

bedroom   kitchen   living room

6 Work in pairs and say where you can put these cards in your home.

| *There's a lamp* | *It's a type of music* | *A cup of tea please* | *I eat lots of biscuits* |

Reading and Listening

1 🔊 **2.17** Read and listen to the information about world cinema. Are these sentences true (T) or false (F)?

1 Hollywood makes 4,000 new films every year.
2 The United States makes the most films every year.
3 Asia makes more films every year than North America.
4 South America makes more films than Africa.

2 🔊 **2.18** Listen to a talk about world film production and complete the information below with the missing numbers.

3 Work in pairs. What information do you think is the most interesting?

World average films per year: _____

- Africa 2.5%
- Europe _____%
- North America _____%
- Asia _____%
- South America 3.5%

World cinema ...
not only Hollywood!

Every year, there are around 4,000 new films in the world. Many people believe that the majority of films are from Hollywood, the American film industry. This is not true.

The truth is that many other countries have very important film industries. Mexican cinema, Iranian cinema and Chinese cinema also make lots of films every year.

The biggest film industry is in India. Bollywood is its largest film producer and one of the largest in the world.

Countries that sell the most cinema tickets every year:
China 1,430,000,000
US 1,400,000,000

World Cinema:
some of the most popular non-Hollywood films

Italy *La Vita è Bella / Life is Beautiful* (1997)

China *Ying Xiong / Hero* (2002)

France *Amélie* (2001)

Germany *Das Boot / The Boat* (1981)

Mexico *El Laberinto del Fauno / Pan's Labyrinth* (2006)

India *Monsoon Wedding* (2001)

Glossary

film industry (*noun*) – all the film businesses

the majority (*noun*) – most of the people or things in a group

Grammar

> *Every year,* there are around 4,000 new films in the world.
> *How often* do you go to the cinema?

- to talk about how frequently we do things, use *every + day / week / month / year*
- use *once / twice / three times / four times + a day / week / month / year*
- to ask about frequency, use *How often ...*

1  2.19 Make sentences about world film production with the words. Then listen and check your answers.

1 Brazil / make / seven new films / month
2 India / make / 2.2 new films / day
3 In the US 1,400 million people / buy / a cinema ticket / year
4 year / 1,430 million people go to the cinema / in China
5 The Philippines / make / around 8.7 new films / week

2 Replace the underlined words with the frequency expressions in the box.

every month   every three months
four times a month   once a year
twice a week

1 I watch a DVD with the family <u>on Fridays and on Sundays</u>.
2 I go to the cinema <u>in January, in February, in March, in April ...</u>
3 There are lots of small film festivals in Toronto, but there is one big one <u>every September.</u>
4 I probably see a foreign film <u>four times a year</u>.
5 I read the film reviews section of the newspaper <u>every week</u>.

G Grammar focus – explanation & more practice of frequency adverbs on page 142

Vocabulary and Speaking

1 Complete the phrases with the verbs in the box. There is one that you do not need.

buy   go   read   sit   watch   see

1 _____ the film reviews
2 _____ a ticket
3 _____ the film
4 _____ to the cinema
5 _____ at the front / at the back / in the middle

2 Put the phrases in order to make a trip to the cinema.

3 Work in pairs. Choose four of the questions below. Ask and answer in pairs.

- How often do you go to the cinema?
- Who do you usually go with?
- What day do you go?
- Do you ever go to the cinema alone?
- Do you know any of the films mentioned in the text on page 54? Do you like them?
- Where do you like to sit?
- Do you read film reviews before you go to the cinema?
- Do you talk during the film?

Film & Television

Part 2

Reading
Make a pitch

Pronunciation
/ɪ/ & /iː/

Vocabulary
Adjectives

Writing
Writing a pitch

Reading

1 Read the definition of a *pitch*. Is there a word for this in your language?

> A pitch is a short description to sell an idea. Film producers look at thousands of pitches. They say you can decide if a story is good with a pitch of less than 50 words.

2 ⊘ **2.20** Work in small groups. Read and listen to *Make a pitch*. Check you understand the words and phrases in bold. Use a dictionary to help you.

3 Read the text again and answer the questions for each pitch.
1 Who are the main characters?
2 What is the problem?

4 Do you recognise any of the films?

Pronunciation

1 ⊘ **2.21** Listen and circle the correct alternative in each pair.

/ɪ/	/iː/
rich	reach
live	leave
still	steal

2 ⊘ **2.22** Listen and put these words into two groups: /ɪ/ and /iː/. What are common spellings for /ɪ/ and /iː/?

big	it	kill	office
people	she	ship	

3 Choose one of the pitches from Reading exercise 2 and present it to a partner. Pay attention to the /ɪ/ and /iː/ sounds.

I have a great idea for a film. Do you want to hear my idea?
In this film ...

4 Which is the best idea for a film? Which is the best pitch?

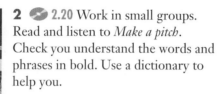

Make a pitch

A rich girl meets a poor boy. They **fall in love**. The girl decides to leave her rich boyfriend. She and the boy are happy. But wait. This story happens on the world's most famous **ship** in history – the Titanic.

A woman **steals** money from her office and **runs away**. She stops for the night at a hotel. The hotel **manager** is a strange man. The hotel is **empty**, and the woman is alone.

On the **coast** of California there is a very big **shark**. It kills people. Three men go out in a **boat** together. They want to kill the shark.

A **spaceship** answers an SOS call from another spaceship. The other spaceship is empty. They continue their journey. But now there is a new passenger on the ship. It is an alien. And it is **hungry**.

Vocabulary

1 Look at the people in the pictures above. What types of film are they watching?

2 Complete the definitions with words in the box. There is one word you do not need.

boring	exciting	funny	sad	scary

thriller: a book, play or film that tells an _____ story

science fiction film: a film about an imaginary future that often includes space travel

romantic drama: a story about love. These films are sometimes _____ and make you cry.

cartoon: an animated film. Cartoons are often _____ and make you laugh.

horror film: a _____ film. It often includes the supernatural.

3 🔊 **2.23** Listen and check your answers. What type of films are the films in Reading exercise 2?

4 Think of examples of ...
- a scary film.
- a funny actor.
- a sad film.
- a boring film.

5 Work in pairs. Read your examples to your partner. Can your partner guess the category?

Writing

Work in pairs and choose **one** of the tasks below.

A Think of a famous film. Write a pitch in no more than 50 words but don't write the name of the film. Give your pitch to another pair. Can they identify your film?

B Look at the pictures. Choose one picture and think of an idea for a film. Write the pitch for your film in no more than 50 words. Present your pitch to other pairs.

Part 3

Vocabulary

1 Look at the screens a–c in the picture below. Which types of television programme in the box go with each screen?

> a comedy programme   a documentary
> a film   a sports programme
> a TV series   the news

2 Look at the other types of programmes in the box. Name an example for each one. Use a dictionary to help you.

3 Work in pairs. Choose three questions and ask your partner. If they say *Yes*, ask the additional question.

Do you watch ...
1. the news? What time / channel?
2. documentaries? What kind?
3. sports programmes? Which sports?
4. comedy programmes? What's your favourite show?
5. films? What type?
6. a TV series? Which one?

A: *Do you watch sports programmes?*
B: *Yes, I do.*
A: *Which sports?*
B: *I watch football every Saturday.*

Listening

1 🔊 2.24–2.28 Listen to five people answering questions from Vocabulary exercise 3. Complete the table.

	Question	Does he /she like this type of programme?
Speaker 1	*4*	
Speaker 2		
Speaker 3		
Speaker 4		
Speaker 5		

2 Listen again and put the sentences in the correct order.

- I don't often watch the news.
- I sometimes watch football with people from work.
- I sometimes watch documentaries about history.
- I watch films in bed because they're always on late.
- I never watch comedy programmes.

Grammar

*They are **always** on late.*
*I **don't often** watch the news.*
*I **never** watch comedy programmes.*

- to talk about frequency in general, use *always, often, sometimes, not often, never*
- the order is usually subject + adverb + verb
- with *be* the order is subject + verb + adverb

1 Match a sentence on the left to a sentence with a similar meaning on the right.

1. I always watch the news on TV.
2. I often watch the news on TV.
3. I sometimes watch the news on TV.
4. I don't often watch the news on TV.
5. I never watch the news on TV.

a. I watch the news on Mondays, Wednesdays and Fridays.
b. I don't watch the news.
c. I watch the news five days a week.
d. I watch the news every day.
e. I watch the news once or twice a week.

2 Add frequency adverbs to these sentences so they are true for you or your country. Then compare your answers with a partner.

1. I watch an American series on TV.
2. I watch films with my friends.
3. The news is on at 8.00pm.
4. I watch documentaries about animals.
5. Football games are on TV on Wednesday nights.

G **Grammar focus** – explanation & more practice of frequency adverbs on page 142

Speaking

1 Work in pairs. Use the notes to prepare questions.

> number of TVs in your house?
> number of hours you watch TV every week?
> watch the news on TV?
> watch TV at dinner?
> record programmes?

2 Write two more questions with your partner.

3 Work with a different student. Ask each other the questions. Remember to use frequency adverbs and try to give some extra information in your answers.

A: *Do you watch TV in bed?*
B: *No, I don't. I never watch TV in bed because I don't have a TV in my bedroom.*

Film & Television

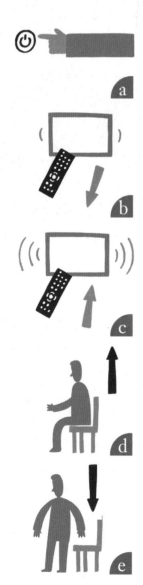

Vocabulary and Pronunciation

1 Match the phrasal verbs in the box to the pictures.

> sit **down**   stand **up**   turn **down**
> turn **off**   turn **up**

2 🔊 **2.29** Listen and check. Notice how we stress the words in bold.

3 🔊 **2.30–2.32** Read the three dialogues and circle the correct phrasal verb. Then listen and check your answers.

1

S = Student   T = Teacher

T: *Turn up / Turn off* the TV, please.

S: Sorry? What?

T: It's very quiet. Can you *turn up / turn off* the TV?

S: Oh, OK.

2

T = Tom   M = Mrs Humphreys

T: Hello, Mrs Humphreys.

M: Oh, hello, Tom. Are you here to see Georgina?

T: Yes.

M: She's at the shops. *Sit down / Stand up* and watch some TV. Would you like a drink?

T: No, thank you.

3

M = Mother   C = Chris

M: Hello? Oh, hi. Wait, just a second … Chris!

C: What?

M: The TV!

C: Yes?

M: *Turn down / Turn up* the TV! I can't hear the person on the telephone.

4 Read the dialogues from exercise 3 together. Choose one dialogue and memorise it with your partner. Then practise saying it.

Reading

1 Check you understand the words in the box. Which words can you use to finish this sentence?

Television makes you …

> crime   effects   fat   headache   hurt
> intelligent   lazy   society   violent

2 🔊 **2.33** Read and listen to *Television theories* on page 61 and check your answers to exercise 1.

3 Look at the sentences below. Match each sentence to a television theory. There is one theory you do not need.

We have a two-year-old baby. She loves these programmes, and they are so good for her!

I don't want to go to the city centre at night. The news says there are lots of problems there.

If I watch television for more than an hour, it hurts my head.

My brother watches television all day. He doesn't want to do anything else.

Turn off the TV and do some exercise! You watch too much television.

Extend your vocabulary – *see, watch*

You *see* with your eyes.
I can see your house from here.
If you *watch* something, you look at it for some time because it is moving or changing.
I watch TV every night.
Work in pairs. Make a list of …

- at least four things you can see from the classroom window.
- at least three sports people watch in your town.

Speaking

Work in pairs. Choose **one** of the tasks below.

A Prepare a dialogue between two people watching television. Include one or more of the phrases in the box in your dialogue.

> It's scary. Please … It's very quiet.
> Sit down. There's nothing on.
> Turn down the volume. What's on tonight?

B Look at the television theories again and mark your opinion next to each one.
1 = strongly disagree, 5 = strongly agree.
Then work in pairs and compare your answers. Try to give reasons.

Useful phrases

- What do you think?
- I agree that …
- For example, there are lots of … programmes on television.
- I disagree, I think that …

Top TV watchers

Country	Number of hours of TV per person per week
1 US	28
2 UK	28
3 Italy	27
4 Germany	23

Television theories

There are many theories on the effects of television on human beings. Here are some of them:

> Television is chewing gum for the eyes.
> Frank Lloyd Wright, American architect

The 'Television makes you stupid' theory This theory says that there are many bad programmes on television. If you watch a lot of these programmes they make you stupid and lazy. You don't think for yourself.

The 'Television makes you fat' theory Some studies say that if people watch too much television they get fat. In the United Kingdom and the United States, many people think that children are fat because they watch lots of television and don't go out to play.

The 'Television makes you intelligent' theory Today there are special series with names like *Baby Einstein*, or *Brainy Baby*. They say that if babies sit down to watch these programmes they develop more quickly.

The 'Television makes you frightened' theory Every day people see crime on documentaries or the news. This theory says that this scares people. They think the world is more dangerous than it really is.

The 'Television makes you violent' theory This theory says that young people are violent because they see violence on television. Some people say that modern video games also make young people violent.

The 'Television makes you ill' theory Some people believe that if you watch television for too long, it hurts your eyes. Some people say that television gives them headaches too.

Function globally shopping

a **electronics shop**   b **gift shop**   c **music store**   d **supermarket**

Warm up

1 Look at the items in the box. Where do you buy them? Match each item to one of the shops above. There may be more than one possible answer.

batteries	CDs	drinks	DVD player	DVDs
flowers	food	fridge	postcards	radio
souvenirs	stereo	T-shirts	television	

2 Use the words in exercise 1 to help you describe the pictures.

Useful phrases

- There are lots of these stores in my country.
- This is an electronics shop. It sells …
- Music stores are open every day. They sell …
- Supermarkets don't open on Sundays.

Listening

1 2.34–2.36 Listen to three conversations. Match each one to a picture. There is one picture you do not need.

2 Listen again and answer the questions.

Conversation 1: What does the man want?
How much does it cost?
Conversation 2: What kind of film does the man want?
How does he want to pay?
Conversation 3: What does the man buy?
How much does it cost?

3 2.37 Listen to the man talking to his wife at home. What is the problem?

Language focus: shopping

1 Match the questions to the possible answers.

1 Can I help you?
2 Can I pay by credit card?
3 How much does this cost?
4 Would you like a bag?

a £4.00
$10.99
b Yes. Where are the televisions?
No, thank you. I'm only looking.
c Yes, please.
No, thank you.
d Yes, of course.
Sorry, cash only.

2 2.38 Listen and check your answers. Practise the expressions.

Speaking

Work in pairs. Choose **one** of the tasks below.

A Test each other on the expressions in the Language focus. A: ask a question. B: give an answer. Close your books and continue. Add new answers.

B Choose one of the shops in the pictures. Prepare a conversation in that shop. Use the language from the lesson to help you.

Global voices

Warm up

Work in groups. Find out the following information quickly. Use the questions to help you.

Which person in the group …
- goes to the cinema the most?
  (*How often do you go to the cinema?*)
- likes Hollywood films?
  (*Do you like Hollywood films?*)
- has the most DVDs at home?
  (*How many DVDs do you have?*)
- watches films on television the most?
  (*How often do you watch films on television?*)

Listening

Leslie, Switzerland   Ryusuke, Japan   Bérangère, France

Key, Hong Kong   Mireille, US

1 🔊 2.39–2.44 Listen to six people answering the question *How often do you go to the cinema?* Circle the correct option.

1	Leslie, Switzerland	*once a month / three times a month*
2	Ryusuke, Japan	*once a month / twice a month*
3	Berangere, France	*two or three times a month / never*
4	Key, Hong Kong	*once a week / once a month*
5	Gloria, Ghana	*twice a month / once every two months*
6	Mireille, US	*once a month / once a year*

2 Listen again. Put the phrases in the order you hear them.
- I sometimes go and see action, sometimes I see comedies ___
- mainly we watch some western movies ___
- sometimes in winter there are many good films ___
- to improve my English I go to the cinema in Oxford ___

Language focus: *it depends*

1 Read the language note. Do you have a similar phrase in your language?

> **Language note:** the phrase *it depends* is very common in spoken English.
> Use it when you can't give a definite answer because different things are possible in different situations.
> *I go to the cinema maybe once a month.* **It depends** *a little on the season because sometimes in winter there are many good films.*

2 Match the questions 1–4 to the answers a–d.
1. Are there any good restaurants near here?
2. Do you like American films?
3. How much are the tickets?
4. How often do you use English at work?

a. It depends. The seats at the front of the cinema are more expensive.
b. It depends on the film.
c. It depends. Some days I don't need to speak English.
d. It depends. Do you like fast food?

Speaking

1 Read the questions. Choose three and think of an answer. Begin your answer with *It depends*.
- How often do you go to the cinema?
- How often do you see your family?
- How often do you walk to school or work?
- How often do you eat in a restaurant?
- How often do you speak English?

2 Work in pairs. Ask and answer the questions.

Reading

1 Read Guncharosh's review of a film and answer the questions.

1 What kind of film is it?
2 Did she like the film?
3 Does it have a happy ending?

I saw a film called *Mamma Mia* recently.

It is a musical and the setting is a beautiful Greek island. The film fantastic, and the story is interesting for everyone. The actors excellent and the songs in the film really great. Some of the singing terrible but it is not a problem.

The story great fun. At the beginning of the film, a pretty young girl called Sophie plans to get married. She has got a mother called Donna but she doesn't know her father. Sophie wants to find her father. She looks in her mother's diary and invites three men (called Sam, Bill and Harry) to the wedding. Donna happy to meet the three men again but she doesn't know who is Sophie's father. At the end of the film Donna falls in love with Sam again. They get married.

It is a very good film and I really recommend it.
I hope you enjoy it!

2 Are these sentences true (T) or false (F)?

1 Donna is not married at the beginning of the film.
2 Sophie finds her father.
3 Donna falls in love with Sam.
4 There is a wedding at the end of the film.

3 What is the film like? Write the adjectives Guncharosh uses to describe these things.

1 The film   *fantastic*, _____
2 The story   _____, _____
3 The songs   _____
4 The singing   _____
5 The actors   _____
6 The setting   _____

4 Do you know this film? If so, do you agree with Guncharosh? Why / why not? If not, would you like to see the film? Why / why not?

Writing skills: using *is* and *are*

Remember to use *is* or *are* before an adjective or noun.

*The film **is** a musical. Sophie **is** a young girl.*
*Sophie and Donna **are** not married.*

Guncharosh sometimes forgets to use *is* and *are* in her review.

She wrote: *The film fantastic* ✗

The correct sentence is: *The film is fantastic* ✔

Find five other places where Guncharosh forgets to use *is* and *are*.

Language focus: *and* and *but*

1 Underline eight places in Guncharosh's review where she uses *and* or *but* to join sentences.

2 Complete the sentences with *and* or *but*.

1 It is a science fiction film _____ it is very interesting.
2 The actors are terrible _____ the music is fantastic.
3 Everyone says it's a great film _____ I want to see it.
4 At the end, they fall in love _____ get married.
5 The film is quite sad _____ it has a happy ending.

Preparing to write

Work in pairs. Tell your partner about a film you saw recently. Use the useful phrases to help you. Do you recommend the film?

Describing a film

- It's a thriller / cartoon / romantic drama.
- The setting is beautiful / an island / an imaginary future.
- The film is fantastic / good / boring / funny.
- The story is interesting / great fun / sad / scary.
- The music is really great / quite good / terrible.
- The actors are excellent / brilliant / not very good.
- At the beginning of the film, …
- At the end of the film, …

Writing

Write a review of a film. Write three paragraphs.

Paragraph 1: Start with *I saw a film called … recently*. Say what type of film it is.
Paragraph 2: Tell the story of the film
Paragraph 3: Say if you recommend the film

Global review

Grammar

1 Put the words in the correct order to make sentences.

1 you the go often cinema to how do?
2 bed sometimes to go I 11.00 at.
3 news often the don't I on watch TV.
4 films ever you do fiction watch science?

2 Correct the mistake in each sentence.

1 I go to the gym once in a week.
2 I drink coffee two times a day.
3 My grandparents visit me every months.
4 I go to a restaurant four time a month.

Vocabulary

1 Decide which word or phrase in each group is different. Why is it different?

1 violence   thriller   cartoon   romantic drama
2 documentary   DVD   sports programme   TV series
3 funny   ill   exciting   scary
4 review   ticket   the news   cinema

2 Complete the sentences with the verbs in the box.

sit down	stand up	turn down	turn off	turn up

Can you stand up, please? I can't see you.
1 The music is very quiet – _____ the radio.
2 _____ and have a cup of tea.
3 I can't hear you – _____ the TV.
4 This programme is boring – _____ the TV.

Speaking and Writing

1 Work with a partner. Write four questions about leisure time beginning with *How often do you ...?* or *Do you ever ...?*

How often do you go to a restaurant?
Do you ever play video games?

2 Work with another pair. Ask them your questions and write down their answers. Tell the class their answers.

3 Work in small groups. Tell your group if you agree or disagree with these statements and say why.

• Romantic dramas are boring.
• TV in my country is very good.
• Going to the cinema is too expensive.
• Bollywood films are very popular in my country.

Study skills

Making notes

1 Answer the questions.

1 How often do you make notes in your English class?
   a always   c sometimes
   b often   d never
2 Where do you make notes?
   a on pieces of paper   c in an exercise book
   b in your coursebook
3 What do you write?
   a words   c answers to exercises
   b grammar notes   d homework

2 Work in pairs and compare your answers.

3 Look at two sets of notes. How are they different?

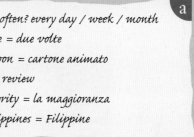

a

how often? every day / week / month
twice = due volte
cartoon = cartone animato
film review
majority = la maggioranza
Philippines = Filippine

b

17ᵗʰ May
How often do you go to the cinema?

go to the cinema	once		week
watch a film on television	twice	a	month
buy a DVD	three times		year

4 Are your notes similar to a or b? How?

5 Read how one student uses her notes.

I read my notes every day after class. I usually read them again at the weekend.

Sometimes I write new words in a vocabulary notebook.

6 Work in pairs. Tell your partner how and when you use your notes.

Work & Study

Part 1

Vocabulary & Reading
Jobs

Listening
Benefits at work

Grammar
Can (possibility)

Writing
Writing about a job

Vocabulary and Reading

1 Complete the jobs by writing the first letter of each one.

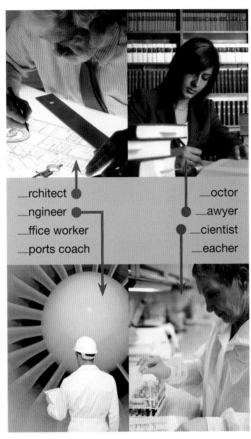

_rchitect _octor
_ngineer _awyer
_ffice worker _cientist
_ports coach _eacher

2 🔊 **2.45** Work in pairs. Read and listen to *The Gallup survey* and look at the jobs in exercise 1. Which five jobs do you think are the most popular with American teenagers?

3 Look at page 130 for the results. Are you surprised by the information? Why do you think these jobs are popular?

4 Look at the expressions with the verb *work*. Add the expressions in the box to the correct group.

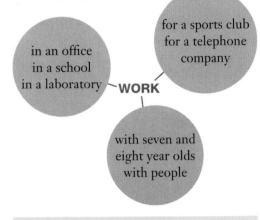

in an office
in a school
in a laboratory

for a sports club
for a telephone company

WORK

with seven and eight year olds
with people

for a bank	for a multinational
in a hospital	in a shop
with animals	with computers

5 Use the expressions to write two or three sentences to describe one of the jobs in exercise 1. Read your sentences to a partner. Can they guess the job?

A: *She works for a medical research company. She works in a laboratory.*

B: *A scientist!*

6 Work in pairs. Choose **one** of the tasks.

A Tell your partner about where you work and the things you do at work.

B Tell your partner about a job you would like to do.

The Gallup survey

Gallup is an organisation started by the American statistician, George Gallup. It finds out about public opinion by asking questions.

In the first Gallup Survey of Young People in 1977, the most popular boys' jobs were carpenter and electrician. For girls, the top job was secretary.

More recently, Gallup asked 1,000 teenagers in the US 'What job would you like to do?'

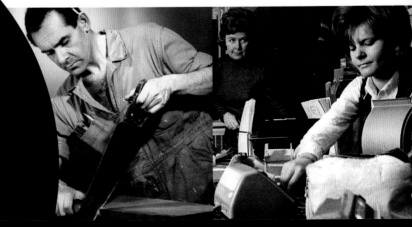

Listening

1 Look at this list of benefits workers get in some companies. Work in pairs and answer the questions.

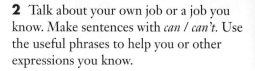

company car   *free meals*
health insurance   holidays
pension   **training**

- Which benefits are usual in your country?
- Which three benefits do you think are the most important?

2 🔊 **2.46–2.49** Listen to four people talking. What are their jobs? Use words from Vocabulary exercise 1 on page 66.

best

worst

3 Listen again and complete the table with the best and worst things about each job.

	Best things ✔	Worst things ✗
1	✔ working with children ✔	✗
2	✔ ✔ company car	✗
3	✔ ✔ pension	✗ long hours
4	✔ free car-parking ✔ sports facilities ✔	✗

4 Which job would you like? Why? Compare with your partner.

Grammar

> *I **can** use all the sports facilities.*
> *We **can't** make personal phone calls.*
> ***Can** you park your car easily at work?*

- use *can* + verb to talk about possibility
- we form the question by putting *can* before the subject
- *can* doesn't change in the third person

1 Read a description about the best and worst things about another job. Find and correct three mistakes with the use of *can*.

My brother's a paediatrician, a children's doctor, in a big hospital in our home town. He loves his job because he cans help children who are ill and their families. But he says sometimes it's very sad when they're very ill and he don't can do anything. And he normally works at night so he doesn't like the hours – he can't to have a normal social life.

2 Talk about your own job or a job you know. Make sentences with *can* / *can't*. Use the useful phrases to help you or other expressions you know.

I can't write personal emails.

Useful phrases

- use a company car
- use the phone for personal calls
- eat for free
- get professional training
- walk to work
- start and finish later some days

ⓖ Grammar focus – explanation & more practice of *can* on page 142

Writing

1 Write a paragraph about your job or a job you know well.

2 Work in small groups and swap your paragraphs. What job(s) would you like?

Work & Study

Part 2

Reading
Ten facts about ... typing

Grammar
Can **(ability), adverbs**

Pronunciation
Can

Vocabulary
Abilities

Reading

1 Work in pairs. Ask each other these questions.

- How often do you use a computer?
- Do you use a computer for work or study?
- Can you type?

2 You are going to read a text about typing. Before you read, check you understand the words and phrases in the box.

average	hurt	keyboard
medical condition	thumb	work skill

3 2.50 Read and listen to *Ten facts about ... typing* and mark each fact with one of the symbols below. Then compare with a partner.

✔ I knew this before.

✘ I didn't know this before.

! This is interesting.

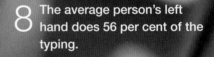

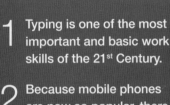

1 Typing is one of the most important and basic work skills of the 21st Century.

2 Because mobile phones are now so popular, there is a new kind of typing – *thumbing*. Thumbing means using one or more thumbs to press the keys.

3 The average person can type between 20 and 35 words per minute. Advanced typists can work very quickly, at more than 110 words per minute.

4 The most common international English keyboard is QWERTY. It gets the name from the first six letters on the top left side of the keyboard. It is more than 130 years old.

5 Other keyboards include QWERTZ (in Germany and Central Europe) and AZERTY (in France and Belgium).

6 Languages with non-Roman alphabets, for example Arabic, Russian, Chinese or Japanese, have their own keyboards.

7 The sentence *The quick brown fox jumps over the lazy dog* is often used to practise typing because it uses every letter of the English alphabet.

8 The average person's left hand does 56 per cent of the typing.

9 Thumbing and typing can hurt you. RSI (repetitive strain injury) is the name of a medical condition you get if you type too much.

10 The 19th-century German philosopher, Friedrich Nietzsche used a typewriter to stop his migraines.

Ten facts about ... **typing**

Glossary

migraine *(noun)* – a very bad headache

Grammar

> He **can** drive.
> **Can** you speak English **well**?
> I **can't** type very **quickly**.

- use *can* with another verb to talk about ability
- add an adverb to say how you do the activity. For most adverbs, add *-ly*. Some adverbs are irregular, eg *good – well*

1 Look at the list of work skills and tick (✔) the ones you can do.

Essential work skills for the 21st century

Can you …
use a computer?
find information on the internet?
work with other people?
type?
learn new things?

English and the world of work

Can you …
understand instructions?
answer the phone and write emails in English?
read texts about your work in English?
translate texts from English into your language?
speak with your colleagues in English?

2 Make the adverb from the adjective in brackets.

I can type …
  easily. (*easy*)
1 _____. (*quick*)
2 _____. (*good*)
3 _____. (*slow*)
4 but not very _____. (*easy*)
5 but not very _____. (*good*)
6 but very _____. (*bad*)

3 Choose five phrases from the boxes in exercise 1 and make sentences about you.

I can work with other people easily.
I can type, but not very quickly.
I can't answer the phone in English.

4 Compare your sentences with a partner.

ⓖ Grammar focus – explanation & more practice of *can* on page 142

Pronunciation

1 🔊 2.51 Read and listen to these quotes about work. What do you notice about the pronunciation of *can*?

One machine can do the work of fifty ordinary men. No machine can do the work of one extraordinary man.
Elbert Hubbard

I like work. I can sit and look at it for hours.
Jerome K Jerome

2 🔊 2.52 Read the rules. Listen and repeat the examples.

- in questions and affirmative sentences, *can* is normally unstressed and we say /kən/
  I can type. Can you?
- in negatives *can't* is produced in the full form
  I can't drive a bus.
- in short answers, *can* is normally stressed and we say /kæn/ and /kɑːnt/
  Can you swim? Yes, I can.

Vocabulary

1 Match the abilities in the box to the pictures.

dance   draw   drive
play a musical instrument   sing   swim

2 Work in pairs. Ask each other questions about the abilities in exercise 1.

a

b

c

d

e

f

Vocabulary and Speaking

1 🔊 **2.53** Look at the different types of schools below. Put them in the order you attend them. Then listen and check your answers. Say the words.

UK	US
primary school	elementary school
nursery school	kindergarten
university	college
secondary school	high school

2 Match the places 1–5 to the descriptions a–e.

1 medical college
2 law school
3 library
4 boarding school
5 technical college

a You can study to be a doctor here.
b You can borrow books and CDs here.
c You can study a specific skill here.
d You can live at this school.
e You can study to be a lawyer here.

3 Look at the graph. Does anything surprise you?

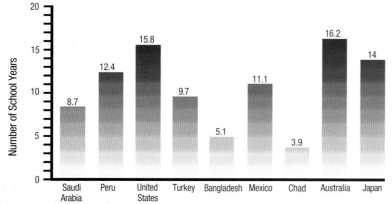

Average number of years children go to school

Number of School Years

Saudi Arabia: 8.7
Peru: 12.4
United States: 15.8
Turkey: 9.7
Bangladesh: 5.1
Mexico: 11.1
Chad: 3.9
Australia: 16.2
Japan: 14

Source: UNESCO & International Literacy Institute

4 Work in pairs and discuss these questions.

• How many years do children go to school in your country?
• How long is a school year?
• What are the best schools in your town? What are the best universities in your country?

Reading and Listening

1 🔊 **2.54** Read and listen to *Important firsts ... centres of learning* on page 71 and complete the first part of the table about Al Karouine.

	Al Karaouine		University of London
Name	Al Karaouine		University of London
First			distance learning programme
Where			
When		3rd century BC	
Extra information	one of the most important education centres for Islamic studies	information on pieces of paper, called scrolls	

2 🔊 **2.55–2.56** Listen to a lecture about two other important centres of learning and complete the rest of the table.

Grammar

> It **was** one of the first universities.
> There **weren't** any books.
>
> - *was / were* is the past form of the verb *be*
> - use *was* with *I / he / she / it*
> - use *were* with *you / we / they*
> - form the negative with *not*

1 Complete the text about Harvard University with *was / were*.

Harvard University _____

the first university in the United States. It was founded in 1636. Harvard has many famous alumni (ex-students). More than 40 Nobel prize winners _____ Harvard University graduates. Seven presidents of the United States _____ students at the university, as well as former prime ministers of Canada, Pakistan, Jamaica, Singapore and Greece.

2 Look at the names of famous teachers in history. Write down as many sentences as you can in two minutes with the words in the circles.

3 Look at page 130. Which of your sentences from exercise 2 were true?

G **Grammar focus** – explanation & more practice of *was / were* on page 142

Isaac Newton
Albert Einstein
Galileo Galilei and
Maria Montessori
Aristotle and Plato
Confucius
Paulo Freire

Italian
Chinese
English
Greek
Brazilian
German

was
were
wasn't
weren't

Important firsts ...

centres of learning

The University of Al Karaouine was founded in the city of Fes, Morocco in 859. It was a mosque, and one of the first universities. The university still exists today and it is now one of the most important education centres for Islamic studies.

Work & Study

Part 4

Vocabulary & Speaking
School subjects

Pronunciation
Two-syllable words

Reading & Listening
School days

Grammar
Questions with was / were

Speaking
Talking about school

Vocabulary and Speaking

1 Match the subjects 1–9 to the things you study a–i.

1 maths
2 biology
3 chemistry
4 history
5 PE (physical education)
6 ICT (information and communication technology)
7 geography
8 physics
9 languages

a French, English, German, Japanese
b football, hockey, basketball, gymnastics
c $(a + b)^2 = a^2 + 2ab + b^2$
d countries, continents, oceans, mountains
e plants, animals
f $e = mc^2$
g 1066, 1492, 1939–1945
h H_2SO_4, H_2O, CO_2
i Word, Excel, PowerPoint

> **Language note:** we use expressions with *be* + adjective + preposition to talk about abilities and interest.
> *When I was at school I **was good at** languages.*
> *My daughter **is interested in** art.*
> ***I was terrible at** sport.*

2 Work in pairs. Read the language note and look at the subjects in exercise 1 again. Without speaking, write five sentences about your partner.

I think you were very good at history when you were at school.
I don't think you were good at maths.

3 Read your sentences to your partner. Were you right?

4 Discuss these questions.

- Do you have all these subjects in your country?
- Do you study any other subjects in your country?
- Which foreign languages do people study in your country?
- Which do you think are the three most important subjects for young people today?

5 Read the information in the box. How would you answer the questions?

Foreign languages ... important to know?

In a recent study of people across Europe, people answered these questions:

Is it important for your children to learn other languages?

93% said yes

Is it important to know another language?

72% said yes

Can you speak more than one foreign language?

26% said yes

Pronunciation

1 🔊 **2.57** Listen and repeat the words. How many syllables do the words have? Which is the stressed syllable?

physics   English   language

2 Find examples of two-syllable words like this in the classroom.

table, teacher, pencil ...

Lindsay Clandfield and **Kate Pickering** are English teachers and writers. He is from Canada and she is from England. They are the authors of *Global Elementary*.

❶ _____

Kate: North London. It wasn't very near my house.

Lindsay: My school was in Canada, in Toronto.

❷ _____

Lindsay: My school was a bilingual school. Half my school subjects were in French and the other half were in English.

Kate: It was an all-girls school. Some of the first women doctors, lawyers and engineers in Britain were at my school.

❸ _____

Kate: A long time! From the age of 7 to 18.

Lindsay: I was at this school for five years, from 13 to 18 years old.

❹ _____

Lindsay: My favourite subject was English. My least favourite subject was maths. It was boring and I wasn't very good at it.

Kate: My favourite subject was German. The teacher was very good. My least favourite? Physics! I wasn't very good at science and I was terrible at physics.

❺ _____

Kate: Yes – it was a good school with opportunities to do other things – art, music, theatre and sports. I had a good time.

Lindsay: Yeah. The school was a bit rough and sometimes a bit scary. But the teachers were good. I still have some friends from that school, which is a bit unusual 20 years later.

Reading and Listening

1 Work in pairs. Think of some answers to these questions.

- Were you happy at school?
- How long were you at the school?
- What type of school was it?
- Where was your school?
- What was your favourite and least favourite subject?

Were you happy at school?

Yes, I was. / No, it was horrible. / It was OK.

2 Read Lindsay and Kate's answers to the questions above. Then write the questions in the correct positions in the text.

3 2.58 Listen and check your answers.

4 Read the statements and circle the correct option.

1 *He / She* was at school in North London.
2 There were two languages at *his / her* school.
3 *He / She* was at this school for 11 years.
4 *He / She* was bored in maths classes.
5 *He / She* has friends from *his / her* schooldays.

Extend your vocabulary – a (little) bit

The expressions *a bit* and *a little bit* are informal. They mean the opposite of *a lot*.

The school was a bit rough and sometimes a bit scary.

Work with a partner. Think of …

- a television show that is a little bit boring.
- a restaurant in your town that is a bit expensive.
- some English grammar that is a bit difficult.
- a film that is a bit sad.

Grammar

Were you happy at school?
Where was your school?

- use *was / were* + subject for yes / no questions
- use a wh- question word + *was / were* + subject for other questions

1 Put the words in the correct order to make questions. Then answer the questions.

Confucius Where born was ?

Where was Confucius born?

1 Plato from and Where Aristotle were ?
2 and Where Maria Montessori when born was ?
3 a Isaac Was Newton scientist ?
4 Brazil Who in 1921 in born was ?
5 German teacher and scientist Which born in 1879 was ?

2 Look at page 130 and check your answers to exercise 1.

Ⓖ Grammar focus – explanation & more practice of questions on page 142

Speaking

Work in pairs. Ask about school. Use the questions from Reading and Listening exercise 1 to help you.

a   b   c   d

Warm up

Look at the pictures of different types of meetings. Where are they? Describe the pictures.

Useful phrases

- I think this is in …
- It's in a …
- (Perhaps) this is a photo of …

Useful language

- an office
- business meeting
- an interview
- a staff meeting
- a class
- the boss

Listening

1 2.59–2.61 Match the situations below to a picture above. Then listen to three conversations from different meetings and match them to the situations.

- in a classroom
- in a business meeting
- in the boss's office

2 Listen again. Circle the correct option.

Conversation 1: The *man / woman* has to send some emails.
Conversation 2: The *man / woman* has a new job.
Conversation 3: The *man / woman* takes the photo.

Language focus: making requests and responses

1 Put the words in order to make requests or responses.

1 finish please Can quickly we ?
2 your books open please you Can ?
3 the door close you Could ?
4 sorry No, I'm .
5 ten minutes in to finish like I'd .
6 of Yes, course .

2 2.62 Complete the table below. Use the sentences in exercise 1 to help you. Then listen and check.

Requests

_____ I / we Could I / we I'd _____ to	finish quickly talk about the next thing	please? please.
Can you _____ you	close the door take our photo explain it again	

Responses

Yes, of _____. Sure.
No, I'm _____ but …

3 Make requests with the words in brackets.

use your pen (I)

Can I use your pen please? Could I use your pen please?

1 help me with my homework (you)
2 finish early today (we)
3 have a cup of tea (I)
4 close the window (you)
5 use that dictionary (I)
6 explain that again (you)

Speaking

Work in pairs. Choose **one** of the tasks below.

A Practise making the requests from Language focus exercise 3. One person asks, the other responds. Then swap roles and repeat.

B Choose one of the meetings in the warm up. Prepare a dialogue. Include two or three requests. Read your dialogue.

Global voices

Warm up

1 Answer the question below. Write two or three sentences.

Who was your favourite teacher at school?

My favourite teacher was …

He/she was interesting/nice/friendly/intelligent …

His/her lessons were …

2 Work with a partner. Read your sentences to each other.

Listening

Matteo, Italy   Eva, Switzerland   Carmen, Spain

Christina, Germany   Bea, England

1 🔊 **2.63–2.67** Listen to five people answering the question *Who was your favourite teacher at school?* Tick (✔) the kinds of teachers you hear.

Ancient Greek teacher	English teacher
French teacher	German teacher
History teacher	Mathematics teacher

2 Listen again and circle the correct option.

1 Matteo, Italy: His favourite teacher was in *high school / elementary school*.

2 Eva, Switzerland: Her favourite teacher was *young and interesting / interested in young people*.

3 Carmen, Spain: Mathematics was really *easy / difficult* with her favourite teacher.

4 Christina, Germany: *The teacher was / the lessons were* inspiring.

5 Bea, England: Her favourite teacher was in *primary / secondary* school.

Language focus: *I think* and *I think that*

> **Language note:** *I think* is one of the most common expressions in English. Use it to give an opinion or say something you think is true.
> You can use *I think* at the beginning or end of a sentence.
> ***I think*** *my favourite teacher was my English teacher.*
> *My favourite teacher was my English teacher,* ***I think***.
> You can also use *I think that* at the beginning of a sentence.
> ***I think that*** *my favourite teacher was my history teacher.*

Choose the correct sentence.

1 a I think is a very good school.
  b I think it is a very good school.

2 a I think that education is important.
  b Education is important, I think that.

3 a I think that my history teacher was my favourite teacher.
  b I think that was my history teacher my favourite teacher.

Speaking

Work in pairs. Choose **three** topics and tell your partner your opinion.

- a very good school in your city
- your worst teacher from the past
- a very difficult subject to learn
- an interesting fact in this book
- a boring subject at school

Reading

Read the job advertisement and Tania's job application letter. Then answer the questions.

1 What job does she want?
2 Where does she work now?
3 Do you think she can do the job well? Why / why not?

Waiter / waitress required for busy waterfront coffee bar.

Previous experience and knowledge of foreign languages desirable.

Apply to: Des Vines, Café Coco, Level 2, Novotel, Sydney Brighton Beach.

Hello, my name is Tania Pedroso and I'd like to apply to be a waitress in your coffee bar.

I'm 25 years old and I'm from Portugal. My parents have a small café in Oporto and I often help them. Now I'm in Sydney. I work in an ice cream parlour three evenings a week but I'd like a full-time job.

I believe I can do this job very well. I can speak three languages – Portuguese, Spanish and English. I can work quickly and I'm good at making different types of coffee (for example espresso, cappuccino, latte). I'm friendly and I like meeting people. I'm also hard-working and efficient.

Please write soon,

Yours sincerely,

Tania

Writing skills: writing a formal letter

1 Read about how to write a formal letter.

a Start the letter with *Dear* ..., **not** *Hello* or *My name is* ...
b Start with the reason for writing the letter.
c Do not use contractions (*it's, don't*).
d Finish with *I look forward to hearing from you.*
e Write your full name at the end.

2 Which of the things a–e does Tania do?

3 Correct Tania's letter.

Language focus: skills and personal qualities

1 Circle the correct option.

1 I am good *at / in* cooking.
2 I *am / have* a driving licence.
3 I like *work / working* with children.
4 I can *use / using* Excel.
5 I *am / have* hard-working.

2 Match the words in the box to the descriptions.

creative   efficient   friendly   patient   reliable

1 You can trust me. _____
2 I don't get angry quickly. _____
3 I like meeting people. _____
4 I'm good at drawing and making things. _____
5 I work quickly and do things well. _____

Preparing to write

1 Work in pairs. Choose one of the jobs in the box to apply for in an English-speaking country.

an au pair   a bus driver   a cook   an office worker
a sports coach   a tourist guide

2 Look at the skills and personal qualities below. Choose three important ones for the job you chose. Can you think of some others?

Describing skills and personal qualities

• I can drive / speak three languages / work quickly.
• I am good at cooking / looking after children / cleaning.
• I am friendly / efficient / creative / patient / reliable / hard-working.
• I like meeting people / sports.
• I have a driving licence / experience of working in bars.

Writing

1 Write an application for the job. Use the useful phrases to help you. Write three paragraphs. Remember to start and finish the letter correctly.

Paragraph 1: Reason for writing the letter
Paragraph 2: Personal information
Paragraph 3: Skills and personal qualities

2 Work in pairs. Compare your letters. Can you make any corrections?

Global review

Grammar

1 Write sentences about what Henry can and can't do at work.

sports facilities ✔ *He can use the sports facilities.*

1 company restaurant ✔   4 no company car park ✗
2 personal phone calls ✗   5 professional training ✔
3 company gym ✔

2 Complete the dialogue with *was, were, wasn't* or *weren't*.

A: What _____ your favourite subject at school?
B: My favourite subjects _____ music and art.
A: _____ you good at English?
B: No, I _____ terrible. But that's because the lessons _____ very interesting.

Vocabulary

1 Find six school subjects in the grid.

O	Y	C	A	H	L	D	R	I	S
C	B	O	J	G	S	H	L	Y	C
E	I	D	R	E	R	B	E	T	H
T	O	M	U	O	R	M	N	G	I
P	L	A	N	G	U	A	G	E	S
I	O	P	A	R	E	T	H	A	T
P	G	U	L	A	T	H	U	N	O
A	Y	T	I	P	A	S	T	E	R
L	V	I	N	H	T	O	U	S	Y
T	A	P	H	Y	S	I	C	S	E

2 Decide if the statements are true (T) or false (F). If they are false correct them by changing the underlined words or phrases.

1 An engineer works in a laboratory.
2 A multinational is a big company.
3 A doctor works with animals.
4 You can buy books and CDs in a library.
5 Children go to primary school before nursery school.
6 An architect can draw well.
7 High school in the US is called secondary school in the UK.
8 Children live at a technical college.
9 You can study to be a doctor at a law school.
10 A piano is a type of job.

Speaking

1 Work in groups of three. Ask questions about abilities starting with *Can you …?*

Find three things that …
• everybody can do well.
• everybody can do, but not well.
• nobody can do.

2 Think of a job. Say what you can and can't do. The other students in the group guess the job.

Study skills

Learning grammar

1 Work in pairs. Write down the page numbers in *Global Elementary* where you can find these things.

• the Grammar focus explanations for units 1 and 2
• the Grammar focus practice for unit 5
• the Grammar focus explanation for *can*
• the Grammar focus exercises for *was / were*

2 Read sentences 1–4 and find an example of each type of word below.

1 Does he work for a big company?
2 There's a lot of milk in the fridge.
3 English people speak quickly.
4 Do you like bananas? I love them.

verb	*speak*
adjective	_____
adverb	_____
preposition	_____
article	_____
countable noun	_____
uncountable noun	_____
pronoun	_____
auxiliary verb	_____
quantifier	_____

3 Work in pairs and compare your answers. Can you think of another example of each type of word?

4 Tick (✔) the sentences which are true for you.

⋆ I enjoy learning grammar.
⋆ I study grammar rules at home.
⋆ I use a grammar book.
⋆ I make grammar notes.
⋆ I do practice exercises at home.
⋆ I practise grammar on a computer.
⋆ I write true sentences to practise grammar.
⋆ I study homework corrections.

5 Work in pairs and compare your answers. Write one new activity you can do to practise grammar.

Part 1

Reading & Listening

The news ... from local to global

Grammar

Past simple (regular verbs)

Writing

A biography

ALLIES' DRASTIC ARMISTICE TERMS TO HUNS

The Daily Mirror

HOW LONDON HAILED THE END OF WAR

Reading and Listening

1 Make these sentences true for you. Then compare with a partner.

1 I buy a newspaper *every day / three times a week / once a week*.
2 I *always / sometimes / never* read the news in English.
3 I *listen / don't listen* to the radio in the morning.
4 I prefer to *read a newspaper / watch the news on TV*.
5 I *always / sometimes / never* read the news on the internet.

2 Read the introduction to *The news ... from local to global* about important events in radio and TV news.

3 Read the rest of the text. Then in pairs, decide when each event happened. Write the decade (1920s, 1970s, etc) on the left. They are in the order they happened.

4 3.01 Listen and check your answers. Write the exact year on the right.

The news ... from local to global

150 years ago there was no radio or television. People read about the news in newspapers, or heard information from neighbours or visiting friends. Now news travels in seconds. Here are some of the most important dates in the history of global news.

Decade	Event	Exact Year
1850s	Paul Reuter used the telegraph to send news and financial information in Europe.	1851
____	Station 8MK in Detroit presented the first radio news programme.	____
____	The BBC World Service radio started.	____
____	The BBC started its first foreign language radio service – in Arabic.	____
1960s	AT&T (American Telephone & Telegraph) launched Telstar into orbit. It was the first active TV and communications satellite.	____
____	600 million people watched Neil Armstrong on the moon.	____
____	A newspaper in Ohio, US produced the first digital newspaper on the internet.	____
____	Ted Turner created the Cable News Network (CNN) on TV, the first 24-hour news channel.	____
1990s	Al Jazeera, the first 24-hour Arabic news station started in Doha, Qatar.	____

Grammar

1 Look at *The news … from local to global* text again and circle the verbs. What do you notice about the spelling?

> *Al Jazeera* **started** *in Doha.*
> *8MK* **presented** *the first radio news*
> *programme.*
>
> • use the past simple to talk about completed actions in the past, usually at a specific time
> • these time expressions are common with the past simple: *yesterday*, *last week / month / year*, *two years ago*

2 Read about another international news channel and write the verbs in the past tense.

> **Channel News Asia**
>
> In the late 1990s MediaCorp _____ (*decide*) to create the first pan-Asian news channel and in 1999 they _____ (*start*) Channel News Asia. A recent survey _____ (*study*) the CNA audience and _____ (*discover*) that 52 per cent of business professionals in Singapore regularly _____ (*watch*) the station.

3 Rewrite the headlines in the past tense. Start with the words in brackets.

> **Police officers at Dublin airport stop four mafia leaders** (yesterday)
>
> **The Boston Symphony Orchestra play final concert of their European tour** (last night)
>
> **The President visits Harvard University and discusses politics with student leaders** (two days ago)
>
> **Teachers demand more money from the government** (last Monday)
>
> **More people study English than any other language** (last year)

G **Grammar focus – explanation**
& more practice of the past simple on page 144

Writing

1 Read *Good night and good luck* about Ed Murrow. Why was he famous?

Good night and good luck

Ed Murrow was one of America's most popular newsreaders. He was born on 25 April 1908 in North Carolina. He studied at Washington State College and when he finished he moved to New York. He married Janet Brewster in 1935 and in the same year started work at CBS (the Columbia Broadcasting System). In the 1950s millions of Americans watched his nightly news programme. His last phrase every night was 'Good Night and Good Luck'. Always a heavy smoker, he died of cancer in 1965.

2 Look at the text again. Complete the sentences with an appropriate preposition. Then underline an example from the text.

Time
for decades use ___*in*___
for complete dates use _____
for years use _____

Place
for institutions use _____
for countries and states use _____
for movement to a place use _____

3 You are going to write your own mini autobiography, but in the third person (*he / she*). Use the ideas below to help you. Write 50 to 100 words but don't write your name on the text.

Useful phrases

> • He / She was born in … (place) in (year)
> • He / She studied (subject) at (school)
> • He / She lived in (place) and worked in (place)
> • He / She married (person) in (year)

4 Give your text to your teacher. Read the autobiographies of other students in the class. Can you guess who they are?

News & Weather

Part 2

Reading & Listening

The Watergate scandal

Grammar

Past simple (irregular verbs)

Pronunciation

The past simple

Speaking

A news story

Reading and Listening

1 Read the information below about the book *All the President's Men* by Woodward and Bernstein. Do you know the story of the Watergate scandal?

All the President's Men is the name of a book by the news reporters, Carl Bernstein and Bob Woodward. It tells the story of the Watergate scandal, a big political scandal in the United States. The reporters discovered that Richard Nixon, the American president at the time, spied on the opposition, the Democratic party. The Woodward and Bernstein news story ended Nixon's Presidency.

Chapter One

June 17, 1972. Nine o'clock Saturday morning. Woodward answered his phone. It was the city news editor of *The Washington Post*. That morning, the police had arrested five men at Democratic headquarters. The men had cameras and electronic equipment. The city editor wanted to know: could Woodward come into the office? Woodward left his apartment and walked to the offices of *The Washington Post*. The newsroom was usually quiet on Saturday morning. Saturday was a day for long lunches and reading the weekend newspapers. Not today. At the front of the newsroom Woodward heard some more news about the burglary. It wasn't at the small local Democratic Party office, but the main headquarters in the Watergate office. That's interesting, he thought.

Woodward picked up the phone and made some calls. He looked across the room and saw Bernstein, another reporter at *The Post*. Carl Bernstein always knew a good story when he saw one, and often got his name on it.

Front page news: President Nixon resigns 9 August, 1974.

2 You are going to read an extract about the Watergate scandal. Check you understand the words in the box.

arrest   burglary
Democratic party (US politics)
editor   headquarters

3 🔊 3.02 Read and listen to the extract from chapter one of *All the President's Men*. Then using the words in exercise 2, tell a partner what it is about.

4 Read the text again. Are these sentences true (T) or false (F)?

1 Woodward phoned the editor at nine o'clock on Saturday morning.
2 The editor wanted Woodward to come to the office.
3 The newsroom was usually busy on Saturday mornings.
4 Woodward thought the burglary was unusual.
5 Woodward didn't know Bernstein.

5 Do you know any other stories or films about reporters? What are they?

Extend your vocabulary – *history* and *story*

History is the study of the past and a subject we study at school. It's normally an uncountable noun.

A *story* is a description of events. It is something we read or something we tell to entertain people.

Choose the correct word.

1 I'm very interested in the *history / story* of Ancient Egypt.
2 We talked to the police, but they didn't believe our *history / story*.
3 My nephew studied American political *history / story* at university.
4 When I was a child, my dad always read me a *history / story* before I went to bed.
5 My brother's a *history / story* professor at York University.

Glossary

a scandal *(noun)* – a situation, often when someone famous does something dishonest

reporters *(noun)* – people who write stories for newspapers

spy *(verb)* – to watch somebody secretly

Grammar

> Woodward **answered** his phone.
> The men **had** cameras.
> Woodward **left** his apartment.

- some verbs are regular in the past simple and finish *-ed*
- other verbs are irregular, *have – had, leave – left*

1 Look at the verbs in the box. Are they regular or irregular? Check in the text, then write the past form.

answer	get	have	hear	know
leave	look	make	pick up	see
walk				

2 Complete the sentences with the past form of the verbs in brackets.

1 Woodward and Bernstein _____ (*be*) two Washington news reporters.
2 They _____ (*hear*) about a burglary at the Democratic headquarters.
3 They _____ (*go*) out and _____ (*ask*) people questions.
4 They _____ (*write*) about it in *The Washington Post* newspaper.
5 The story _____ (*get*) bigger and bigger.
6 It _____ (*become*) a scandal for the United States government.
7 The story _____ (*end*) Richard Nixon's presidency.
8 In 1976 they _____ (*make*) a film from the book.
9 Robert Redford and Dustin Hoffman _____ (*be*) in the film.
10 The film _____ (*win*) four Oscars.

3 🔊 **3.03** Listen and check your answers. Say the sentences.

Ⓖ **Grammar focus** – explanation & more practice of the past simple on page 144

Pronunciation

1 🔊 **3.04** Listen to how the infinitive and the past form of these verbs are pronounced. Repeat the words.

answer – answered
wait – waited
stop – stopped
look – looked
end – ended
listen – listened
start – started
walk – walked

2 Underline the correct word to complete the rule.

- if a regular verb ends in *-ted* or *-ded* pronounce / *don't pronounce* an extra syllable

3 Work in groups. Take turns and read the extract from *All the President's Men* aloud. Pay attention to the past tense verbs.

Speaking

1 Work in pairs. Write down …

1 the name of a person you know.
2 a restaurant or hotel you know.
3 a food.
4 a topic of conversation.
5 another topic of conversation.
6 a question.
7 an answer.
8 a time.
9 the name of a newspaper.

2 Now turn to page 131 and complete the news story with the words from exercise 1.

3 Work with another pair. Tell each other your news stories.

Bob Woodward, left, and Carl Bernstein were in their 20s when they began investigating the Watergate story.

Front page news: President Nixon resigns 9 August, 1974.

a

b

c

d

e

Vocabulary

1 Match the words to the pictures.

> clouds   rain   snow   sun   wind

2 Read the language note, then complete the sentences with the correct form of the word in brackets.

> **Language note:** to make the adjective of these weather words, add -*y*: *wind – windy*

It was _windy_ yesterday. (*wind*)
1   The _____ season is from July to October. (*rain*)
2   Children don't go to school if the weather is _____. (*snow*)
3   It was _____ this morning when I got up. (*cloud*)
4   If it's _____ at the weekend, many people go to the beach. (*sun*)

3 Put the words in order from cold to hot.
• cold
• freezing
• hot
• cool
• boiling
• warm

4 What's hot for you? What's cold for you? Decide on a temperature range for each word. Compare with a partner. Then turn to page 131 to see what someone from Jordan and someone from Siberia think.

Reading

1 Read the sentence. Do you think it's true (T) or false (F)?

Eskimos have more words for snow than other people.

2 🔊 3.05 Read and listen to *The great Eskimo vocabulary hoax* on page 83. Then choose the correct answer to exercise 1.
a   The sentence is true.
b   The sentence is false.
c   It's impossible to say.

3 Read the text again and match the two parts of the sentences below.
1   Whorf believed that Eskimos had different words for snow because
2   The number of Eskimo words for snow
3   Many people don't like
4   Lots of languages have many words

a   for snow.
b   the word Eskimo.
c   grew and grew.
d   they see snow differently.

4 How many words for snow are there in your language?

Grammar

> Native people don't use <u>the word Eskimo</u>.
> They don't like **it**.
>
> **It's** sunny today.
> **It's** six o'clock.

- use *it* to replace singular nouns
- we also use *it* to talk about the weather and to talk about the time

1 What does *it* refer to in the sentences? Use the words in the box. There is one word you do not need.

| a linguist   blizzard   Inuit or Aleut   sleet |
| slush   The great Eskimo vocabulary hoax |

<u>It</u> is a more correct word for Eskimo.
Inuit or Aleut

1   <u>It</u> is the story of how the number of Eskimo words for *snow* grew.
2   <u>It</u> is a mixture of snow and rain.
3   <u>It</u> is the English word for a snowstorm.
4   <u>It</u> is a kind of snow that is part snow and part water.

2 The conversations below are missing the word *it* four times. Complete them by putting *it* in the correct places.

1
A: Excuse me, what time is?
B: Oh, is ten past six.
A: Thanks.

2
A: Is this your car?
B: Yes, is.
A: It's very nice.

3
A: Would you like to go to the park?
B: Now? Is cold and rainy.
A: Oh.

3 🔊 **3.06–3.08** Listen and check your answers.

Ⓖ **Grammar focus –** explanation & more practice of *it* on page 144

The **great Eskimo vocabulary hoax**

Do Eskimos really have more words for snow?

How many words do the Eskimos have for snow? In 1911, one book said there were four words. Some years later, another book said there were seven. In 1940 Benjamin Whorf, an American linguist, said that Eskimos have different words for snow because they see snow differently.

Over the years the story continued, and the numbers grew. Some books said that the Eskimos had a hundred words for snow, others said thousands. So, how many are there really? The truth is there isn't an easy answer to the question.

First of all, there isn't only one Eskimo language, there are many. Also, native people of the Arctic don't use the word *Eskimo*. They don't like it. They call themselves *Inuit* or *Aleut*. And finally, having words for different types of snow really isn't unusual: there are many words for snow in other languages too. In English, for example, we have *sleet* (a mix of snow and rain), *slush* (part snow, part water) or a *blizzard* (a snowstorm) and others.

Linguists call Whorf's idea *The great Eskimo vocabulary hoax.* So the next time someone tells you that Eskimos have 1,000 words for snow, tell them it isn't true!

Speaking

Work in pairs. Choose **one** of the tasks below.

A Read the conversations from Grammar exercise 2 together.

B Change some information in the conversations from Grammar exercise 2. Then read them together.

C Choose two conversations from Grammar exercise 2. Read each one together and then try to continue it.

> **Glossary**
>
> **a hoax** *(noun)* – a trick in which someone tells people that something is true when it is not true
>
> **a linguist** *(noun)* – someone who studies and speaks a lot of languages

Part 4

Speaking

1 Complete the sentences with your opinions, using the type of word indicated in brackets.

- I hate _____ days. (weather adjective)
- I love it when it's _____. (weather adjective)
- In my country, the best weather is in _____. (place)
- My favourite time of year is _____. (month)

2 Work in pairs. Compare your sentences.

A: *I love it when it's sunny.*

B: *Why?*

A: *Because we go to the beach.*

Reading and Listening

storm /stɔːm/ (*noun*) when a lot of rain or snow falls very quickly, often with very strong winds or thunder and lightning

1 Read *Storm chasing* on page 85 and look at the pictures. Which two pictures describe it?

2 🔊 3.09 Now read *Storm chasing* again and complete the text with the phrases below. Then listen and check your answers.

1 Last August.
2 Because a friend invited me.
3 In France.
4 My friend Daniel.
5 Really, really scared.
6 Well the most important thing was a specially converted car.

a

b

c

Grammar

> *Why did* you *go* storm chasing?
> *Did you have* any special equipment?
> I *didn't* really *know* anything about storm chasing.

- use the auxiliary *did* to make questions and negatives in the past simple
- for questions the structure is (*Wh*-question word) + *did* + subject + infinitive
- for negatives the structure is subject + *didn't* + infinitive

1 Rewrite these sentences about the text so they are true.

1 Alan knew a lot about storm chasing the first time.
2 Alan went with his girlfriend Joanne.
3 They chased the storm in a bus.
4 The car had lots of metal.
5 Lightning hit the car twice.

2 Correct the questions.

1 Where did go you?
2 Who you go with?
3 How did you travelled?
4 What did you there?
5 Had you a good time?

G Grammar focus – explanation & more practice of the past simple on page 144

Pronunciation

1 🔊 3.10 Which word is pronounced differently? Listen and circle the word.

1 why   what   when   who   where
2 how   hotel   hour   house   hungry

2 Complete the sentences with words with the same sound.

1 Last **W**ednesday, the **w**eather **w**as

   _____.

2 **H**arry **h**as a _____.
3 **W**illiam **w**orks _____.
4 **H**ello! **H**ow are you? I'm _____.

3 Work in pairs and swap your sentences. Read them aloud.

Storm chasing: a great day out?

We normally use the expression *a great day out* when we go somewhere for fun. But Alan's day out was very unusual – and maybe *fun* isn't the right word!

What is storm chasing?
Storm chasing is when people go out in bad weather. They want to get very, very near to a storm and take photos of extreme weather conditions.

Why did you go storm chasing?
_____ This friend, well he did it all the time and said it was amazing. I didn't really know anything about storm chasing.

Who did you go with?
_____ I knew he was a bit crazy but I didn't know how crazy!

When did you go?
_____ We went in the summer – they say it's the best time of year to chase storms.

And where?
_____ Daniel lives near the Pic du Midi in the Pyrenees. It's a great place for storm chasing.

Did you have any special equipment?
_____ It didn't have any metal, but it had lots of plastic and rubber. That protects you from lightning. And you know what? Lightning hit the car three times!

How did you feel?
_____ I mean it was really exciting but it was also the most terrifying experience of my life.

Alan is from London, UK. He often goes storm chasing with his friend, Daniel. He also likes taking photographs and filming videos of storms.

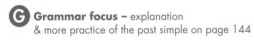

Speaking

Work in pairs. A: turn to page 127. B: turn to page 129. Use the questions in Grammar exercise 2 to ask your partner about a day out.

Function globally speaking on the telephone

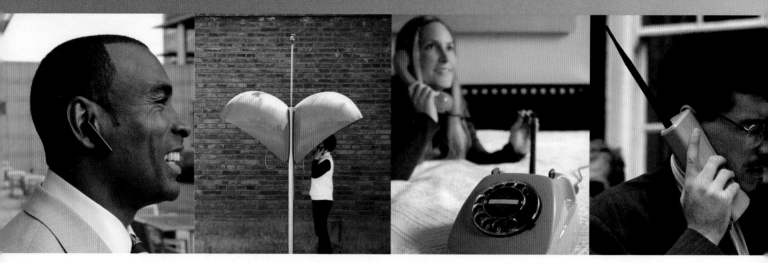

Warm up

1 Put the sentences in the correct order to make a conversation to International Directory Enquiries.

> And what's the name of the city or town you would like to call? ____
>
> P, for Paul. ____
>
> The United States. _2_
>
> Thank you. The number is 312 567 8741. ____
>
> Chicago, Illinois. ____
>
> McGuinness. ____
>
> What country would you like to call? _1_
>
> What is their first initial? ____
>
> What is the last name of the person you would like to call? ____

2 Work in pairs. Read the conversation.

Listening

1 🔊 **3.11– 3.14** Listen to four phone conversations. Match each one to a situation.

a Someone's busy.   c Someone's out.
b One person can't hear well.   d Someone wants to meet.

2 Listen again. Are the statements true (T) or false (F)?

1 The man calls a newspaper office.
2 The man doesn't want to wait.
3 The man has important information.
4 The man has some photos for the woman.

3 What do you think the secret information is? Imagine what is in the photos. Tell a partner.

Language focus: speaking on the telephone

1 Complete the table with the words and phrases in the box.

busy	call	calling	minute	speak to

Hello, Hi,	is that	Susan?
	is	Susan there?
	Liz	speaking.
Can I		Susan?
	leave a message for	
Who's	_____	please?
I'm sorry,	he / she's	_____.
		out.
	you have the wrong number.	
Sure,	just a _____ / second.	
	hold please.	
I'll	_____	you later.
	wait.	

2 🔊 **3.15** Listen and check your answers. Then listen and repeat the phrases. What are the phrases in your language?

Speaking

Work in pairs. Choose **one** of the tasks below.

A Repeat the Warm up exercise. One person is the operator and the other person is calling for information.

B Choose one of the situations from Listening exercise 1. Create a phone conversation. Use some of the expressions from the Language focus to help you.

Global voices

Warm up

1 Put the types of weather in order of preference from 1 (*I love this weather*) to 5 (*I hate this weather*).

a cold, rainy day with clouds ___
a rainy day, but warm ___
a very cold day, but sunny ___
a very hot day, with clouds ___
a warm sunny day ___

2 Work in pairs and compare your answers.

Listening

1 🔊 3.16–3.19 Listen to four people talk about their favourite weather. Which speaker does **not** say the word *sunny*?

1 Haruna, Japan
2 Maida, Switzerland
3 Al-Mutasem, Saudi Arabia
4 Mireille, US

2 Listen again and match the sentences a–e to the speakers 1–4 above. There is one extra sentence.

a I don't like it when it is too hot.
b I go out in sunny weather.
c I obviously prefer it when it's warm.
d If it's cloudy or like windy or snowy I don't go out.
e The weather in Jeddah is always hot.

Language focus: interjections

Language note: in spoken English, people often use *um* and *uh* to give themselves time to think of what they want to say.
I really like, um, sunny, hot weather.

Read what Mireille says about her favourite weather. Then listen again and complete the text with *um* or nothing.

_____ let's see … I love – I like _____ sunny weather but I don't like it when it is too hot. _____ I like it sunny and cool _____ and so I like the English weather for that. _____. In California I like it _____ when it's sunny too but not too hot, but sunny and warm _____ enough to go to the beach.

Speaking

Work in pairs. Take it in turns to finish the sentences below. Don't think too much before you finish the sentence. Use *um* and *uh* to give you time to think.

- My favourite weather is, um …
- Today the weather was, uh …
- When it's sunny outside I often …, um, …
- Summer in my country is never …, um, …

Haruna, Japan   Maida, Switzerland   Al-Mutasem, Saudi Arabia   Mireille, US

Writing describing an event

Reading

1 Read Omar's report on a local event. What is the event and why is it important?

Last week the Sharjah World Book Fair took place in Sharjah, in the United Arab Emirates. *The Sharjah World Book Fair* lasted ten days. *The Sharjah World Book Fair* is famous all over the world. There were over one thousand publishers from many different countries *at the Book Fair*. Thousands of people visited *the Book Fair*.

The Book Fair had lots of different sections, including sections for children's books. Most books were in Arabic, but there were some books in English. Lots of different writers came to the fair. There were several activities for children. There was also a lot of delicious Arabic food.

The Sharjah World Book Fair takes place every year. Sheik Sultan bin Mohammed Al Qasemi, President of Sharjah visits *the Book Fair*. The aim of the Book Fair is to encourage young people to buy and read more books. The books are not usually very expensive.

2 Answer the questions about the report.
1 When did the event take place?
2 Where did it take place?
3 How long did it last?
4 How many people attended?
5 What happened at the event?
6 How often does it take place?
7 What is the aim of the event?
8 What did people buy, sell and eat?

Writing skills: avoiding repetition

Use pronouns (*it, he, him, they*, etc) and *there* to avoid repetition.

1 Replace the underlined words and phrases in Omar's report with *it* or *there*.

2 Replace the underlined words or phrases in these sentences with a pronoun, or *there*.
1 There were many children's books. The children's books were attractive and not expensive.
2 Sharjah is in the United Arab Emirates. The Book Fair took place in Sharjah.
3 The president of Sharjah made a speech. The organiser of the event thanked the President.

Language focus: writing about numbers

1 Complete the sentences from Omar's report.
1 There were _____ publishers from _____ different countries at the Book Fair.
2 _____ people visited the Book Fair.
3 The Book Fair had _____ different sections.
4 _____ books were in Arabic, but there were _____ books in English.
5 _____ different writers came to the fair.
6 There were _____ activities for children.

2 Read the text about an event in Rio de Janeiro, Brazil. Correct the underlined words and phrases.

Last month was the carnival in Rio. <u>Thousand</u> of foreigners visited it. A number of events took place during the day, but <u>the most</u> took place at night. There were <u>severals</u> visitors from all over the world, and <u>lot</u> of fireworks. Over ten thousand people watched the procession and <u>most of</u> people in the town took part in the dancing. It was a great event!

Preparing to write

1 Make notes about an event that took place in your school, place of work, town, or country. Use the questions in the Reading section and the useful phrases to help you.

2 Work with a partner. Tell each other about the event. Use the past tense.

Describing an event
- It took place on / at / in …
- Over a hundred / Thousands of people visited / attended it.
- There were speeches / fireworks.
- There were several sporting events including football, basketball and hockey.
- The aim of the event was to raise money for charity.

Writing

Write about the event. Use your notes to help you.

Global review

Grammar

1 Circle the correct option.

1 Where *you went / did you go / did you went* at the weekend?
2 Who *you went / did you go / did go you* on holiday with?
3 How *did you travel / did you travelled / you travelled* to London?
4 What *did you / did you do / you did* last night?
5 *Did you have / Did you had / Had you* a good time at the party?
6 What time *it is / is / is it*?
7 *Is it / It is / Is* snowy in Alaska in December?
8 Blizzard *is / it is / is it* the English word for a snow storm.

2 Write the past tense of these verbs.

become _____	stop _____	play _____
know _____	win _____	study _____
make _____	hear _____	visit _____
see _____	leave _____	write _____

Vocabulary

Complete the sentences with adjectives to describe the weather.

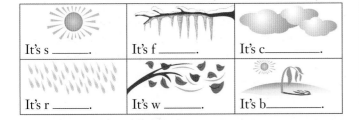

It's s _____.	It's f _____.	It's c _____.
It's r _____.	It's w _____.	It's b _____.

Speaking and Writing

1 Work in pairs. Ask questions about what your partner did …

- before the class.
- last night.
- at the weekend.
- on their last holiday.

Tell the class one thing about your partner.

2 Write three true sentences about the weather using *because*.

I went swimming yesterday because it was sunny.

3 Work in small groups. Read the first half of your sentences to the group. Can they guess the endings?

I went swimming yesterday because …

Study skills

Remembering words

> One way of remembering words is to put them in groups.

1 Work in pairs. Match the word groups 1–5 to the descriptions a–e. Then add two more words from the unit to each group.

1 cool, weather, rainy, _____ , _____
2 left, saw, knew, _____ , _____
3 sometimes, scandal, story, _____ , _____
4 wrote, snow, cold, _____ , _____
5 headquarters, news, arrest, _____ , _____

a They are the same word class (eg noun, verb etc)
b They start with the same letter.
c They are about the same topic.
d They are in the same reading text.
e They have the same sound.

2 Which way of grouping words in exercise 1 do you prefer? Work in pairs and make a word group using words from this unit. Show your list to another pair. Do they understand how you grouped the words?

> You can also remember words by making word associations. For example, one Spanish student remembers snow by thinking of the Spanish word for snow, *nevar*. *Nevar* is similar to *never*. She wrote the sentence: *It never snows in my city*.

3 Make some word associations for English words. Then work in pairs and explain the associations to your partner.

> Spider diagrams are another way of remembering words.

4 Look at the spider diagram. Can you add any words?

5 Work in pairs. Make a spider diagram using *TV* or *weather*. Then show your diagram to another pair. Can they add any words?

Coming & Going

on foot

Vocabulary

1 🔊 **3.20** Listen and repeat the different methods of transport in the box.

> by bicycle / bike   by boat   on foot
> by metro   by motorcycle / motorbike
> by train

Useful phrases

- take the train / the bus / the metro
- travel by train / bus / car / metro / bike
- go on foot

Language note: in London, the metro is called *the underground* or *tube.* In New York, it is called *the subway.*

2 Choose three sentences. Complete them so they are true for you.

- I have a …
- I take … every day.
- I never go by …
- I don't like travelling by …
- When I was young, I travelled a lot by …
- I came … to class today.

3 Compare your sentences with a partner.

Reading

1 Do you have a bike? How often do you travel by bike?

2 🔊 **3.21** Read and listen to *Pedal power* on page 91 about bicycle use in Europe. Which chart goes with the text?

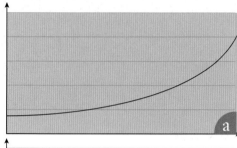

a

b

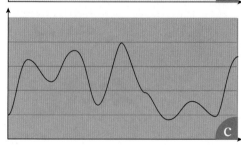

c

3 Read the text again. Are the statements true (T) or false (F)?

1 Julian usually takes his car to work.
2 The bicycles in the Vélib' network aren't expensive.
3 There is one Vélib' station in the city of Paris.
4 Urban bicycle networks are more and more popular in Europe.
5 Julian doesn't like Vélib'.

4 Discuss these questions in pairs.

- Do you think Vélib' and similar projects are a good idea?
- Is there a similar scheme in your city?
- Is bicycle use changing in your area?

train   motorcycle / motorbike   bicycle / bike

boat   metro

Pedal power

Every day, Julian gets up, gets dressed and goes to work in Paris, France. He usually goes by car. This week is different. Julian isn't taking his car, he's going by bike.

Julian is one of Paris's 195,000 users of Vélib', a bicycle hire network which started in 2007. With Vélib', people can go to a special bicycle station and take a bicycle. They take it where they want to go, and leave it at another station. There are thousands of Vélib' stations around the city.

It isn't only in France. Across Europe, projects like Vélib' are becoming more popular. People are travelling more by bicycle and less by car. There are urban bicycle networks in cities in Spain, England, Austria, Germany, Holland, Denmark and Finland. Other countries across Europe are thinking of similar projects.

'It's great. The trip to work is not very long, I feel good and it's cheap.' says Julian.

Grammar

*Today he's **going** by bike.*
*People **are travelling** more by bicycle and less by car.*

- use the present continuous to describe what is happening at this moment or around the present time
- these expressions are common with the present continuous: *now, these days, at the moment, this week / month / year*

1 Find another example of the present continuous in the text.

2 Complete the text below with the present continuous of the verb in brackets.

End of the bicycle kingdom?

The bicycle industry began in China in the 1930s, and soon there were bicycles everywhere. People called China the *Bicycle kingdom*. But now the situation _____ (*change*). The economy _____ (*grow*), and Chinese people _____ (*make*) more money. They _____ (*not buy*) bicycles, they _____ (*buy*) cars. In 2005 there were 20 million cars in China. Now experts _____ (*say*) the number will be 140 million in the year 2020.

3 Make sentences about the graphs. Use the present continuous and one of the verbs in the box.

change	go down	go up

Bicycle use in Europe

Bicycle use in China

G **Grammar focus** – explanation & more practice of the present continuous on page 146

Pronunciation

1 3.22 Read and listen to the words with the /ŋ/ sound.

travelling   going   England   thank you

2 3.23 Listen to the chant and mark the stress.

He's going by bus.
She's catching a plane.
They're taking the car.
I'm going by train.

3 Work in pairs. Practise saying the chant.

Speaking

Read a questionnaire on transport on page 132 and answer the questions.

Coming & Going

Part 2

Vocabulary and Reading

1 Look at the pairs of words. Which is the bigger number in each pair? Write the words in numbers.

1 twenty   twenty-five
2 a thousand   a hundred
3 eight hundred   a hundred and eighty
4 nine thousand   ninety thousand
5 five thousand five hundred   fifty-five thousand
6 one hundred and thirty-five   one thousand and thirty-five

2 🔊 **3.24** Listen and repeat the numbers in exercise 1.

> **Language note:** we say *two hundred*, *two thousand*, **not** ~~two hundreds~~, ~~two thousands~~.

3 🔊 **3.25** Read and listen to *Coming to Hong Kong* about an interesting form of transportation in Hong Kong. Match the numbers to the information.

1 20   a the total distance the escalators travel
2 25   b the number of people who use the escalators every day
3 135   c the time it takes to go up all the escalators
4 800   d the number of escalators
5 55,000   e the vertical distance the escalators go up

Listening

1 🔊 **3.26** Listen to a report about the Mid-Levels Escalators. Who is the commuter – the man or the woman?

2 Listen again and circle the correct option.

1 She's at the *top* / *bottom* of the escalators.
2 The escalators are going *up* / *down* now.
3 *Lots of people* / *Not many people* are using the escalators now.
4 He uses the escalators *once* / *twice* a day.
5 The man *likes* / *doesn't like* the escalators.

Extend your vocabulary – *come* and *go*

In general *come* is used for a movement in the direction of the speaker. We often use it with words like *here* and *this*.

Go is used for a movement away from the speaker. We often use it with *there* and *that*.

Please come in. The doctor can see you now.
Please go away! I'm trying to work.

Complete the sentences with the correct form of *come* or *go*.

1 _____ and look at this video – it's amazing!
2 What time are you _____ home today? Can you finish this report first?
3 We decided to _____ to Scotland for another holiday. We love it there.
4 I want to _____ and live in a hot country.
5 We're having a party on Saturday. Would you like to _____?

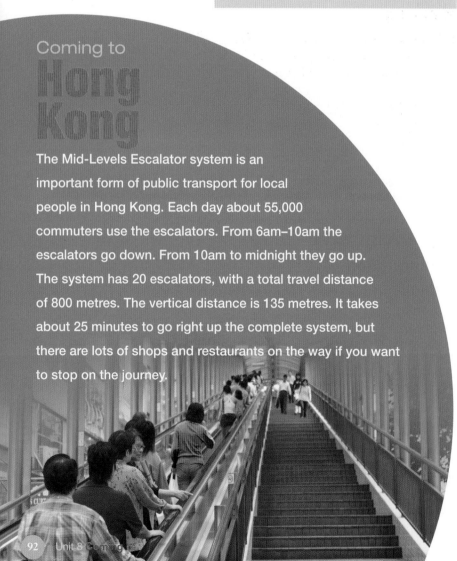

Coming to Hong Kong

The Mid-Levels Escalator system is an important form of public transport for local people in Hong Kong. Each day about 55,000 commuters use the escalators. From 6am–10am the escalators go down. From 10am to midnight they go up. The system has 20 escalators, with a total travel distance of 800 metres. The vertical distance is 135 metres. It takes about 25 minutes to go right up the complete system, but there are lots of shops and restaurants on the way if you want to stop on the journey.

Grammar

> *Every day thousands of people* **use** *these escalators to go to work.*
> *Hundreds of people* **are coming** *in.*

- use the present simple to talk about things which are generally true and habitual actions
- use the present continuous to describe what is happening now or around the present time

1 Read three announcements you hear when you travel. Circle the correct verb form.

Passenger announcements

This is a national bus service information message about bus services from Glasgow to London. On Mondays, Wednesdays and Fridays, the first bus *leaves / is leaving* Glasgow at 5.15am. It *is stopping / stops* at Birmingham and *arrives / is arriving* at London Victoria at 12.35.

Good afternoon ladies and gentlemen. This is flight BA 652 to Milan. If you *are travelling / travel* with babies or small children this morning, please come to the front of the queue.

This is a passenger information announcement. This weekend we *do / are doing* repairs on the blue line. No trains *are travelling / travel* between New Bridge station and South Central station. Passengers who normally *use / are using* this service should change onto the red line at King Street station.

2 **3.27–3.29** Listen and check your answers.

3 **3.30** Complete the dialogue with the correct form of the verb in brackets. Then listen and check your answers.

A: Excuse me. Can you help me?
B: Sure. Where _____ (*you / go*)?
A: I _____ (*try*) to go to West Harrow. It's on the Metropolitan line.
B: OK. Some of the trains on this platform _____ (*go*) there. Trains to Uxbridge _____ (*stop*) at West Harrow but trains to Watford _____ (*not / stop*) there. Look, a train _____ (*come*) now. OK, this is an Uxbridge train. This one _____ (*go*) to West Harrow.

G **Grammar focus –** explanation & more practice of the present simple and continuous on page 146

Speaking

1 Work in pairs. You are going to write a conversation between two people travelling. Choose **one** idea from each box below.

A	a journalist
	a ticket inspector
	a police officer

B	a tourist
	an old lady
	a businessman / woman

C	on the Mid-Levels Escalator
	at an airport
	on the metro

D	'Where are you going?'
	'I'm using the phone.'
	'What are you looking at?'
	'You're not listening to me.'

2 Write your conversation.

3 Work with another pair and read your conversation to them.

a worried   b angry   c happy

d bored

e sad

f nervous

Vocabulary and Listening

1 🔊 **3.31** Look at the pictures and the adjectives to describe how the people are feeling. Listen and repeat the words.

2 🔊 **3.32–3.36** Listen to five conversations at an airport. Circle the correct adjective to describe the people's feelings.

1 He's *angry / bored*.
2 They're *happy / sad*.
3 They're *nervous / happy*.
4 They're *angry / bored*.
5 She's *worried / angry*.

> **Language note:** use *get* + adjective to say we are beginning to feel that way.
> I **get angry** when people use their mobile phones in restaurants.

3 Work in pairs. Choose three of these questions. Ask and answer them.

- Do you get nervous when you fly?
- Do you get angry easily in traffic?
- How do you avoid getting bored on long car or bus journeys?
- Do you get worried before you go on a long journey?

Reading

1 What countries do you know? What countries would you like to visit? Tell a partner.

2 🔊 **3.37** Read and listen to *Culture shock!* on page 95. According to the text, what is the best definition of *culture shock*?

a feeling angry and sad in a new culture
b the stages which visitors to a new culture experience
c the final stage of a visit to a new culture

3 Read the text again. Match the pink words to these definitions.

1 someone from another country
2 gradually
3 a word or phrase
4 for all time in the future, permanently
5 a person who studies human customs and culture

4 Have you ever experienced culture shock? How did you feel?

5 Work in pairs. Look at the tips to avoid culture shock. Are they useful?

English place names

by David Crystal

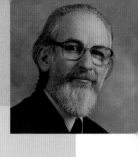

The place names of the English-speaking world give us fascinating linguistic information about history - and perhaps national character
5 too. In the US we find *Washington*, *Jamestown*, *Louisiana*, and thousands more places named after famous people. The modest British don't usually go in for this. There isn't an
10 *Elizabethville* or *Charlesburg* in the UK.

All over the New World, places have the names of important people from history in a way that is very different from Britain. Australia has
15 its *Victoria*, *Cooktown*, and *Gibson Desert*. Important places usually get the names of rulers, statesmen, explorers, soldiers, and sailors but, surprisingly, not the names of
20 artists, writers, and composers. Even *Shakespeare* hardly ever appears in the English place names of the world.

Some place names are very imaginative. *Cape*
25 *Catastrophe* and *Hard Luck Creek*. *Hope Valley* and *Fort Defiance*. *Weary Bay* and *Thirsty Sound*. There's a place called *Hot Coffee* in
30 Mississippi and one called *Difficult* in Tennessee. And in New Mexico, in 1950, the town of *Hot Springs* took the name of a popular radio show, and became *Truth and Consequences*.

Glossary

be named after somebody (*phrasal verb*) - be called the same name as somebody

composer (*noun*) – someone who writes music, especially classical music

fascinating (*adjective*) – very interesting

go in for something (*verb*) – do something

hardly ever (*adverb*) – very rarely

imaginative (*adjective*) – showing new and different ideas

statesman (*noun*) – a political leader that people respect

Warm up

1 Work in small groups. How many place names (of cities, towns etc) do you know in English? Make a list. You have two minutes.

2 Compare your list with other groups in the class. Who has the longest list?

Reading

1 Read *English place names*. Are the sentences true (T) or false (F)?

1 Many places in the United States get their names from people.
2 Many places in England get their names from people.
3 Many places in the New World get their names from people.
4 Many places get their names from artists or writers.
5 Many places get their names from soldiers, sailors or politicians.

2 Read again and match:

1 a place name in the US named after a famous statesman
2 a place name that does not exist in England
3 A name of an important person for Australia
4 Two very imaginative place names
5 A name of a radio show

a Charlesburg
b Difficult
c Gibson
d Hot Coffee
e Truth and Consequences
f Washington

Language

Find words in the place names in the text with the following meanings. The first letter is given. Use a dictionary to help you.

1 t_____ feeling that you want or need a drink
2 c_____ an event that is very bad, a disaster
3 d_____ the opposite of easy
4 w_____ a word that means very tired
5 v_____ an area between two mountains
6 c_____ a very small river

Speaking

Choose one of the questions below and answer it with a partner.

- What are the strangest place names you know? Tell your partner. Make a list.
- Are there places in your country named after statesmen or soldiers? Are there any places named after artists?
- Invent some strange English place names. Use the following words to help you, and add other English words or names. Imagine what kind of place it is.

... -ville   ... -town   Cape ...   Fort ...   ... and ...

Writing A report

Reading

1 Read Sebastian's report about transport in Poland.

Which paragraph mentions …
1 transport in the capital city?
2 travelling to work?
3 travelling between cities?

a In Poland, most people go to work by bus or tram. Buses are very cheap and they are usually punctual. In most towns, people take the tram to go to work or to go shopping. Trams are mostly efficient but sometimes they are quite crowded.

b In Warsaw, many people are takeing the metro these days. It is faster and more efficient than buses. Some people travel by car, but traffic is becomeing heavyer. It takes a long time to get to the city centre and it is difficult to find a parking place. A few people are also useing bikes now but it is very dangerous in the city centre.

c Most people travel between citys by car or by train. Express trains are faster and safer than cars. It takes about three hours to get from Warsaw to Krakow by train. Our main problem is that in Poland there aren't many motorways. Also, there are lots of road works. It is a never-ending problem. However, at the moment we are building new motorways and the situation is geting better.

2 Match the types of transport 1–5 with the descriptions a–e from the report.

1	buses	a	dangerous in the city centre
2	trams	b	fast and safe
3	bicycles	c	cheap and punctual
4	trains	d	slow and difficult to park
5	cars	e	efficient but sometimes crowded

3 What does Sebastian say is changing at the moment?

Writing skills: spelling

1 Read the spelling rules.

a words ending with one vowel + consonant: double the consonant before *er* or *ing*.   *sit – sitting*
b words ending with consonant + *e*: no *e* before *ing*. *make – making*
c words ending with consonant + *y*: change *y* to *i* before *er*, change *y* to *ie* before *s*.   *friendly – friendlier*

2 Find six spelling mistakes in Sebastian's report and correct them. Then match each mistake to one of the rules a–c.

3 Write the correct spellings.

use + ing   *using*
1 busy + er   _____
2 travel + ing   _____
3 party + s   _____
4 big + er   _____
5 change + ing   _____

Language focus: journey times

1 Complete the sentences from the report.
1 It _____ to _____ the city centre.
2 It _____ about three hours _____ Warsaw to Krakow _____.

2 Complete the sentences about your town or country.
1 It takes _____ to get from my house to the city centre by _____.
2 It takes _____ to get from _____ to _____ by _____.

Preparing to write

Work in pairs. Tell your partner about transport in your country. Use the useful phrases to help you.

Writing a report

- Most / many / some / a few people travel by bus.
- People mostly / usually / often / sometimes take the metro.
- These days / Now / At the moment people are going by bike.
- A big problem / Our main problem is that traffic is heavy.
- Car accidents are a serious / never-ending problem.
- The situation is changing / getting better / getting worse.

Writing

Write a report about transport in your country or in another country. Say how people usually travel, and what is changing at the moment. Write three paragraphs.

Paragraph 1: Travelling to work
Paragraph 2: Transport in the capital city
Paragraph 3: Travelling between cities

Global review

Grammar

Circle the correct option.

Hi Jerry

I (1) *write / am writing* this postcard from Geneva! Yes, I arrived here yesterday (2) *to start / for start* my new job. The job is great and people are (3) *friendlier / much friendly* than in my last job. But everything is very different here. The weather is (4) *colder / more colder* than the weather at home and things are (5) *expensiver / more expensive* in the shops. The day (6) *starts / is starting* much earlier here, but public transport is (7) *better / more good* and people (8) *don't usually arrive / aren't usually arriving* late for work, like they do at home. People here (9) *drive / are driving* on the right, so that's a bit strange for me.

Anyway, that's all for now – I (10) *go / am going* out now (11) *to get / getting* the bus to work.

Write soon!
Dan

Vocabulary

1 Complete the sentences with the feelings.

angry   nervous   bored   sad   worried

1 I was very _____ when my dog died.
2 This is my first time on a plane. I'm feeling a bit _____.
3 It makes me very _____ when buses arrive late.
4 I sometimes get _____ on long car journeys.
5 John wasn't on the bus. I'm _____ about him.

2 Circle the correct option.

A: How do you usually get to work?
B: I usually (1) *travel / take* the bus but last week it was very snowy and there were no buses, so I went (2) *on foot / on feet*. What about you?
A: I usually travel by (3) *the bus / bus* too, and I sometimes go (4) *by / in* car. But last week I decided to take (5) *metro / the metro*, because of the snow.

Speaking and Writing

1 Work in pairs. Choose an object and write a sentence to say why you use it. Then read the sentence to the class. Can they guess the object?

You use this to clean your teeth.

2 Work in pairs. What do your friends and family members usually do at this time of day? What are they doing at the moment? Tell your partner.

My mother usually works at home. I think she's cooking at the moment.

Study skills

Understanding learning aims

1 Why are you studying English? Tick (✔) the phrases which are true for you. Then work in pairs and compare your answers.

* to pass an exam
* to communicate with people from other cultures
* to travel to an English-speaking country
* to get a good job
* to understand pop songs
* to have fun
* to live or study in an English-speaking country
* because English is an important international language
* because I enjoy learning languages
* for another reason

2 Read what one student wrote about learning English. Which learning aims from exercise 1 are true for her?

I really enjoy my English classes. There are people from all over the world and I can learn so much from them. I want to learn more English to tell people about my country, and to learn about their countries.

3 What are you doing to achieve your learning aims? Work in pairs and compare your answers.

Understanding the aims of classroom activities can help you learn.

4 Work in pairs and look again at unit 8. Choose the main aim for these activities.

1 Reading about *Pedal power* on page 90
   a   to learn about Vélib'
   b   to improve your reading
   c   to learn new words
2 Speaking on page 93
   a   to improve your grammar
   b   to speak more confidently
   c   to have fun

5 Work in pairs. What are the main aims of these activities?

* Listening on page 92
* Grammar on page 95
* Writing on page 95
* Pronunciation on page 97

Glossary

constantly *(adverb)* – all the time

look up *(verb)* – find

species *(noun)* – a plant or animal group

Vocabulary and Speaking

1 Write the words in the box in the correct categories below.

| bird | fish | flower | insect | lake |
| plant | zoo |

1 park, farm,
_____

NATURE

2 animal, tree,
_____,
_____,
_____,
_____,

3 mountain, river,
_____

2 3.42 Listen and check your answers.

3 Work in pairs. A: turn to page 127. B: turn to page 129. Describe the pictures to your partner.

Reading

1 3.43 Read and listen to *One planet, one place!* What is EOL?

2 In your own words, explain the EOL project. Do you think it's a good idea?

Listening

1 3.44 Listen to two people talking about unusual species. Are they …

a a teacher and a student?
b two friends?
c a reporter and a scientist?

2 Look at the pictures below. Then listen again and answer the questions.

1 Which two pictures do they talk about?
2 Where does the first animal come from?
3 Where does the second animal come from?
4 Has the person used the EOL website before?

One planet, one place!

The Encyclopedia of Life is a project to create an online reference of every living species on earth. Scientists from all over the world are constantly putting information on the EOL website. There are texts, photographs, sounds, videos and maps. Anyone can look up information in the encyclopedia. Scientists hope the project will encourage people to learn more about the planet and protect nature.

The work has started …

Encyclopedia of Life

tarsier

fiddler crab

okapi

red lionfish

Grammar

Some people **have got** tattoos of names of people.
I've got one on my arm.

- use *have got* to talk about possession and family relationships. *Have got* means the same as *have*
- the negative is *haven't got*, and the question form is *Have … got?*

1 🔊 **3.49** Write down the different people and objects you hear. Then write true sentences about you. Use *have got* and *haven't got*.

2 Rewrite the sentences in exercise 1 to make questions. Then work in pairs and ask each other the questions.

A: *Have you got a car?*

B: *Yes, I have.*

No, I haven't.

ⓖ **Grammar focus** – explanation & more practice of *have got* on page 148

Vocabulary

1 🔊 **3.50** Look at the picture of a face. Listen and repeat the words.

The face

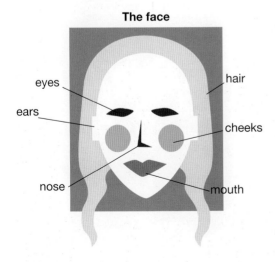

eyes
ears
nose
hair
cheeks
mouth

2 Write the words in brackets in the correct position to complete the descriptions.

1 He's tall and thin. He's got long _____ and very blue _____. (*eyes, hair*)
2 She's got _____ brown eyes and _____ hair. (*big, short*)
3 She's got black _____ and a thin _____. (*face, hair*)
4 He's tall and he's got big _____. He's got a tattoo on his _____. (*leg, ears*)
5 He's _____. He's got black _____. (*hair, short*)
6 Her baby's beautiful. He's got lots of black _____ and lovely big, pink _____! (*cheeks, hair*)

Writing

1 Read the situation below.

A friend or family member is coming from another country to visit you. You can't meet them at the airport. You want your partner to meet them, but your partner doesn't know what they look like.

2 Write a short letter describing your friend or family member. Use the language below and the vocabulary from this lesson to help you.

Hi …
I'm writing to ask if you can help me. My _____ is coming to the airport and I can't be there. Can you meet him? He's _____ and he's got _____.
Thanks!

3 Work in pairs and swap your letters. Read your partner's letter and write a short response.

Sure, I can meet your _____. No problem.

I'm sorry, I can't meet _____. I'm busy then. I've got (a party / work / a meeting).

Part 4

Vocabulary

1 Work in pairs. Can you name the pictures below? Use a dictionary to help you.

2 What's the difference between …
- a shirt and a T-shirt?
- a skirt and a dress?
- a jumper and a jacket?
- a tie and a scarf?
- shorts and trousers?
- gloves and socks?

A shirt is more formal than a T-shirt.

3 Read the language note. Then work in pairs and describe other students in the class. Can your partner guess who it is?

> **Language note:** we use the verb *wear* with clothes.
> *She's wearing a red T-shirt and black trousers.*
> *She usually wears a dress.*

Pronunciation

1 🔊 3.51 Listen and repeat the words in the box.

scarf	shirt	shoe	skirt	sock

2 🔊 3.52 Listen to these words. Circle the first word you hear.

1 see — she
2 so — show
3 sort — short
4 sock — shock

3 Work in pairs. Say a word from exercise 2 to your partner. They point to the word.

4 🔊 3.53 Listen to the tongue twister. Can you say it?

Sam sells Sheena six short skirts.
Shelly shows Susie seven silk shirts.

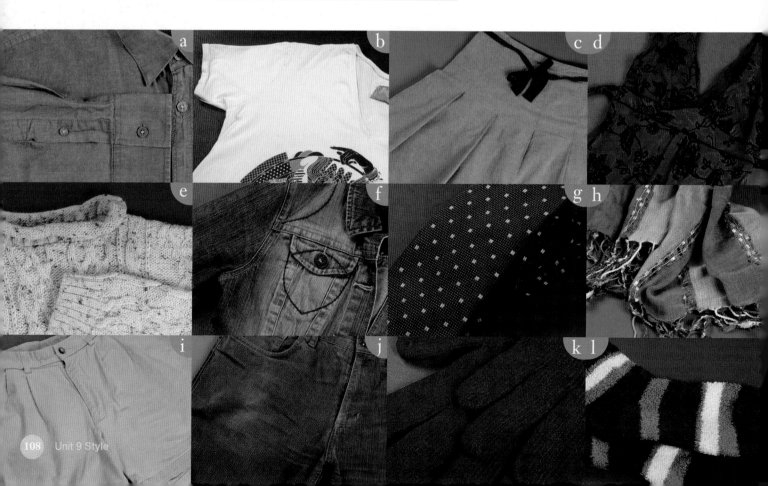

buttons   pockets   printed T-shirt   socks

Listening

1 Work in pairs. Look at the clothing items on this page. Which one do you think is the oldest? The most modern?

I think socks are the oldest.

Maybe the sports shoe is the most modern.

> **Language note:** *sports shoe = trainer* in British English and *sneaker* in American English.

2 3.54 Listen to a lecture about the history of fashion and write the clothing items in the correct position on the timeline.

2000 BC	_____
500 BC	_____
400 BC	_____
1500	_____
the 1860s	_____
1917	_____
1939	_____

3 Choose **two** clothing items. Listen again and make notes. Then compare with your partner. Check your notes with the audioscript on page 157.

4 In your opinion which item of clothing is the most useful? Why?

> ### Extend your vocabulary – talking about colours
>
> We can use the words *light* or *dark* to describe colours in more detail.
> *She is wearing a light green shirt.*
> *He always wears dark blue trousers.*
> Work with another student. Repeat Vocabulary exercise 3, but include *light* or *dark* in your descriptions.

Grammar

> *The first **ones** were for decoration.*
> *They used the first **one** to advertise the film The Wizard of Oz.*
>
> • use *one* (singular) and *ones* (plural) to refer to something you said before
> • we usually use *one* with an adjective, or with *this / that* in front of it

1 Replace the underlined words with an item of clothing from Listening exercise 1.

1 Don't wear white <u>ones</u> with black shoes.
2 I wore one to a wedding last year. It was a big blue <u>one</u>, with flowers on top.
3 These <u>ones</u> are especially for tennis, and those <u>ones</u> are for general sports.
4 I've got some old <u>ones</u> I wear in the garden. They're much more comfortable than the trousers I have to wear for work.

> **Language note:** use *which* or *which one* to ask about something if there aren't many examples.
> ***Which one** is your bag?* (there are only two or three bags)
> ***Which** would you like, tea or coffee?* (there is only tea or coffee)

2 Work in pairs and ask each other about these things in your classroom.

• bag   • pens   • book
• jacket   • phone

A: *Which is Hamed's bag?*
B: *The brown one.*
A: *Which are Galina's books?*
B: *Those ones.*

Ⓖ **Grammar focus –** explanation & more practice of *one* and *ones* on page 148

sports shoes

blue jeans

hat

Function globally talking about health problems

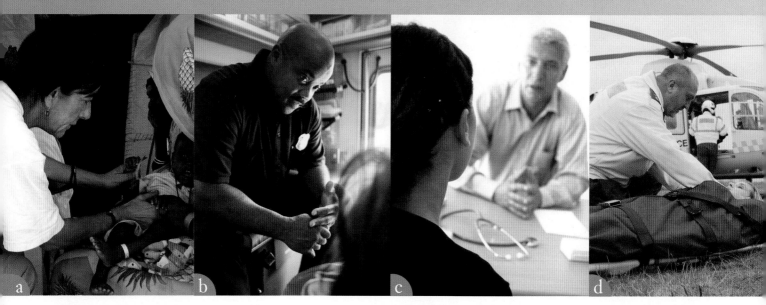

a   b   c   d

Warm up

Work in pairs and look at the four pictures of doctors. Take turns to describe the different pictures.

Useful language

- In the picture I can see …
- There is / are … in this picture.
- This is a picture of …
- … is richer / poorer / easier / more difficult than …
- Maybe they are in Africa.
- He is a doctor perhaps.
- She is helping …
- They are operating …

Listening

1 🔊 **3.55–3.56** Listen to two conversations. Match each one to a picture. There are two pictures you do not need.

2 Listen again. Are these statements true (T) or false (F)?

Conversation 1: The woman fell down.
            Her arm hurts.
            She would like some water.

Conversation 2: Dr Hathaway's office is the second door on the left.
            The man has a headache.
            The doctor thinks the medicine is too strong.

Language focus: talking about health problems

1 Who says it? Read the sentences and mark them *D* for doctor and *P* for patient.

What is the problem? ___
I don't feel well. ___
Where does it hurt? ___
Take this medicine. ___
I've got a headache. ___
You need to go to the hospital. ___
Can I see please? ___
Is it broken? ___
Drink lots of water. ___

2 Make two new sentences with the words in brackets.

I've got toothache   (back, ear)
My finger hurts.   (eye, feet)
I've got a sore arm.   (leg, neck)

3 🔊 **3.57** Listen and check your answers. Point to the part of the body you hear.

Speaking

1 Work in pairs and make up a conversation. Use the example below to help you.

A: Greet the doctor.
B: Greet the patient. Ask what's wrong.
A: Tell the doctor what's wrong.
B: Ask to see.
A: Show the doctor. Ask a question about it.
B: Say no. Give an instruction.

2 Present your conversation to another pair.

English advertising goes to the movies
by David Crystal

Films and advertising are both huge businesses so it's not surprising to see them working together in more and more sophisticated ways. In the past, commercials were an aperitif, something you saw
5 before the movie. Then, people only had to watch several minutes of advertising before the main film started. Today, there's no escape; the ads are also in the film. It's called *in-film advertising*.

Brand props (short for 'properties' – objects for
10 a play or in a film) started in the 1940s. Joan Crawford didn't drink whiskey in *Mildred Pierce* (1948); she drank Jack Daniels whiskey. Today brand props are big business. We see the stars with a specific product, or we see a logo or an ad
15 somewhere in the film.

For a long time, products in films appeared in the background. Today, companies want more; they want *brand fit* – in other words, the product is needed for the story in the film. Look at the cars
20 and watches used by James Bond, and you'll see what I mean.

Glossary

ad (*noun*) - advertisement

aperitif (*noun*) - a drink that you have before a meal

background (*noun*) – the part of the film that is behind the main characters or action

big business (*noun*) – something that makes a lot of money

brand (*noun*) – product that has its own name and is made by one company e.g. Nike, Coca-Cola®

commercial (*noun*) – advertisement

escape (*noun*) – getting away

huge (*adjective*) – very big

logo (*noun*) – a symbol that represents a company or organisation

movie-goer (*noun*) – a person who goes to the movies

sophisticated (*adjective*) – complicated and advanced

Warm up

Look at the definition of a brand. Can you think of two brands for each of the following things?

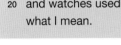

drinks   perfume   watches   cars

Reading

1 Read *English advertising goes to the movies* and match the phrases and definitions.

1 in-film advertising
2 brand props
3 brand fit

a objects in a movie which have a particular brand and are part of the story
b advertising that happens in a film
c objects in a movie which have a particular brand

2 Read the text again. Complete the sentences with a, b or c.

1 Film and advertising …
   a work separately.
   b work together.
   c are in competition.
2 In the past commercials came …
   a before the film.
   b after the film.
   c in the middle of the film.
3 Today, advertising is …
   a separate from the film.
   b more important than the film.
   c in the film.

4 In-film advertising started …
   a in the first half of the 20th century.
   b in the second half of the 20th century.
   c this century.
5 The way products appear in films now is …
   a the same as in the past.
   b different from the past.

Language focus

Look at the words in the box. Which words are connected to advertising (A)? Which words are connected to cinema (C)?

films *C*	ads	product
advertising	props	logo
commercial	brand	background
movie-goer	star	story
main film		

Speaking

Work in pairs and discuss the questions.

- Have you ever noticed *in-film advertising*? Can you think of an example?
- Do you think in-film advertising is a bad thing?
- What type of products do you see in advertisements at the cinema in your country?

Writing a speech

1 Read Giovanna's speech to introduce a visitor to her school. Who is the visitor and why is she important?

Ladies and gentlemen, I would like to introduce a very important visitor. She is one of the most famous scientists in the world. She is also the oldest living person to have a Nobel Prize. Her name is Rita Levi Montalcini. Rita was born in Turin, in Italy. She studied medicine at the Turin Medical School, and later specialised in neurology. In 1986 she won the Nobel Prize for Medicine with an American colleague, Stanley Cohen. Rita has taught in a number of universities all over the world, and has won many prizes. She has made many important discoveries about nerve cells in the brain. Her work has contributed to the treatment of several diseases, including multiple sclerosis and cancer. We are very pleased that Rita can come and talk to us today about her life and work. Ladies and gentlemen, please welcome Rita Levi Montalcini.

2 Complete the table with facts about Rita's life.

Profession	
Background and education	
Prizes	
Work and achievements	

Writing skills: using paragraphs

Paragraphs are groups of sentences which are used to separate ideas in a text.

Divide Giovanna's speech into four paragraphs with these headings.

a why the person is important
b life and background
c achievements
d welcome

Language focus: superlative structures

1 Complete the sentences from the text.

She is _____ in the world.
She is also _____ a Nobel Prize.

2 Complete the sentences with words and phrases in the box.

athletes	environmentalists	to run	explorers
politicians	to become	to reach	to win

1 Wangari Maathai is one of the most important _____ in the world. She is the first woman from Africa _____ the Nobel Peace Prize for her work with planting trees in Kenya.
2 Ranulph Fiennes is one of the most famous _____. He was the first man _____ both the North and South Poles.
3 Barack Obama is one of the most important _____ in the world. He was the first black American _____ President of the US.
4 Thelma Pitt-Turner is one of the most amazing _____ in the world. She is one of the oldest people _____ a marathon. She was eighty-two at the time.

Preparing to write

Make notes about an important person from your country or another country. Use the paragraph headings in the Writing skills section to help you.

Making a speech

- Ladies and gentlemen, I would like to introduce …
- I am very pleased to welcome …
- We are very pleased that he / she can come and talk to us about …
- Please welcome …

Writing

1 Write a speech to introduce the person to your school. Use your notes and the useful phrases to help you. Write four paragraphs using the headings from the Writing skills section.

2 Work in pairs. Exchange your speech with your partner. Check your partner has used paragraphs.

3 Read your speech to other people in the class.

Global review

Grammar

Correct one mistake in each sentence.

1 Have you ever go to China?
2 Mount Everest is highest mountain in the world.
3 A: Can I see that jumper, please?
  B: Which?
4 I don't have flown in an aeroplane.
5 These are the more expensive trousers in the shop.
6 A: Which shoes do you want to try on?
  B: The black, please.
7 Do you got a car?
8 Have you ever took photos in a zoo?
9 A: Which is your house?
  B: It's that next to the supermarket.
10 I haven't a dress for the wedding.

Vocabulary

1 Match words 1–6 to words a–f.

1	head	a	park
2	hands	b	zoo
3	feet	c	gloves
4	tree	d	river
5	fish	e	socks
6	animal	f	hat

2 Complete the sentences with one or more words.

In my country we (1) _____ school at the age of 5, and
(2) _____ school at the age of 18. We normally
(3) _____ from university at about 21 and (4) _____
work. We usually (5) _____ at the age of 65.

Speaking and Writing

1 Work in pairs. Sit back-to-back with another pair and try to describe the other pair's appearance (hair, eyes, clothes). Then turn round and check. Were you right?

2 Write four sentences about your experiences using the present perfect. One must be false. Work in small groups. Take it in turns to read out your sentences and try to guess which one is false.

I've …
I haven't …
I've been to …
I've never been to …

Study skills

Dictionary skills 2: learning about words

A learner's dictionary can give you information about the class of a word (eg noun, adjective, preposition etc). It can also give you other information about the grammar of a word.

Sometimes a word can have two word classes. For example, *plant* can be a noun and a verb.

> plant 1 (*noun*)
> 1 [C] a living thing that grows in soil and has leaves and roots: *a strawberry* **plant**
> plant 2 (*verb*)
> 1 to put trees, plants, or seeds in soil so that they will grow there: *I've* **planted** *a small apple tree in the garden.*

1 Look up these words in a dictionary. Write two word classes and an example sentence for each word.

fish 1 _____
      2 _____
giant 1 _____
      2 _____

A dictionary can tell you if a noun is countable (C), uncountable (U) or both (C/U). For example the dictionary entry above tells us that *plant* is countable (C).

2 Work in pairs. Write C, U, or C/U next to the words. Then check your answers in a dictionary.

art _____   painting _____
information _____   project _____
nature _____   species _____

A learner's dictionary can also tell you the past participle form of a verb.

> swim (*verb*) (past tense **swam**; past participle **swum**)

3 Work in pairs. Write the past participles of these verbs. Then check your answers in a dictionary.

swim   *swum*
break _____   fall _____
drink _____   make _____
eat   _____   sleep _____

Vocabulary and Speaking

1 You are going on a long plane or train journey. Which **two** things below do you take to pass the time?

2 Complete the sentences with a suitable verb.

1 You can d _____   puzzles / sports / nothing

2 You can r _____   books / comics / newspapers

3 You can p _____   video games / board games / cards

3 Which of the activities in exercise 2 do you do in your free time? Complete the sentences and tell a partner.

In my free time I often …

In my free time I sometimes …

In my free time I never …

Reading

1 🔘 3.58 Read and listen to *Masters of fun* on page 115 and match the pictures to the paragraphs.

2 Read the text again and choose the correct answer.

1 Manga books are popular …
   a with adults in America.
   b with young people around the world.
   c with people on buses and trains.

2 You read a Manga book …
   a differently from an English book.
   b from left to right.
   c more quickly than an English book.

3 Sudoku is a popular game …
   a in America.
   b for people on their way to work.
   c only in Japan.

4 Playing video games is …
   a popular with adults.
   b popular in Japan.
   c an American invention.

5 Dr Kawashima's *Brain Training* is …
   a a game for children.
   b a game for adults.
   c a puzzle.

3 Have you ever seen, read or played any of these things?

Extend your vocabulary – *fun* and *funny*

We use *fun* when we have a good time or enjoy ourselves.
I had fun.
We use *funny* if something (a person, film, joke, etc) actually makes us laugh.
It's a very funny film.

Choose the correct word.

1 My brother's always telling jokes. He's really *fun / funny*.

2 That party last week was a lot of *fun / funny*.

3 How was your holiday? Did you have *fun / funny*?

4 Did you see that new comedy programme on TV last night? I didn't think it was very *fun / funny*.

5 We did a new activity in English class today. It was good *fun / funny*.

Grammar

> *Doing* Sudoku is a popular activity.
> Many people **love reading** Manga.

- use the *-ing* form of the verb to describe an activity
- we use the *-ing* form as the subject at the start of a sentence or after verbs *like, love, hate,* etc

1 Make sentences with the prompts. Do you agree?

1 Do / Sudoku / is very difficult.
2 Play / video games / is for young people.
3 Do / puzzles / helps you stay young.
4 Read / comics / is boring.
5 Have / fun / is the most important thing in life.

2 Make three true sentences and one false sentence about the free time activities in Vocabulary exercise 2. Use the verbs below and the *-ing* form.

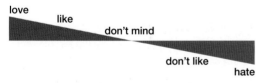

I love doing puzzles.
I don't mind reading newspapers.

3 Work in pairs. Read your sentences to your partner. Can they guess the false sentence?

G **Grammar focus** – explanation & more

Masters of fun

Manga, Sudoku, Brain Age or the popular Playstation® – it seems that everywhere you look, the Japanese are very good at helping people have fun. We take a closer look …

1 **Manga** is the name of a style of Japanese comics. They began in the late 18th century. Many young people around the world love reading Manga but in Japan they are popular with adults and young people. One interesting thing about Manga comics is that – even in English – you read them from right to left, and not from left to right and you start at the back of the book.

2 **Sudoku** is a kind of number puzzle. It was very popular in Japan in the 1990s but it became famous around the world in 2005. You can find Sudoku puzzles now in newspapers almost everywhere. Doing Sudoku is a popular activity for people on the bus or train to work.

3 Playing video games is almost a national pastime in Japan. So it's no surprise that the Playstation and Nintendo® video game companies are Japanese. One of the most recent popular games for adults is **Dr. Kawashima's Brain Training™**. This is a video game with a series of puzzles. Kawashima says that doing these puzzles is good for your health; it makes your brain younger and your thinking time quicker.

Part 2

practice of the -ing form on page 150

Reading and Speaking

1 🔊 **3.59** Look at the pictures. Read and listen to the *Malta fact file*. Find the answers to these questions.

1 Where is Malta?
2 What languages do they speak there?
3 How many people live there?
4 What is the weather usually like?

2 Work in pairs and ask each other the questions.

- Do you know anything else about Malta?
- What do you think are popular activities for people who visit this place?

Vocabulary

1 Look at the pictures of Malta on page 117. Match the words in the box to the pictures.

beach	castle	church
monument	museum	restaurant

2 Read the definitions of different places in a city. Then make similar definitions for the words below. Use a dictionary to help you.

a shop – you can buy things here
a market – you can sell things here
a theatre – you can see plays and operas here

- a hotel
- an airport
- a sports stadium
- an art gallery

Listening

1 🔊 **3.60–3.66** Listen to seven people who are going to visit Malta. Circle the best summary for each speaker.

Speaker 1: *cultural visit / fun in the sun*
Speaker 2: *tourism / business*
Speaker 3: *activities for adults / activities for children*
Speaker 4: *water sports / cultural visit*
Speaker 5: *getting married in Malta / getting married in London*
Speaker 6: *making a film / making a TV show*
Speaker 7: *learning English / teaching English*

2 Listen again and make notes for each speaker. Then compare your answers in pairs. What are each person's plans?

3 Look at the pictures again. What would you like to do in Malta?

Malta fact file

Name: Malta

Location: Southern Europe, island in the Mediterranean Sea

Area: 316 sq km

Population: 403,000

Languages: Maltese, English

Climate: Mediterranean, rainy winters, hot summers

Economy: Electronics, pharmaceuticals and tourism

Gozo
Rabat
Mediterranean Sea
Comino
Malta
Mediterranean Sea
Medina
Valletta

Grammar

> *I'm going to visit the old bits of Malta.*
> *We're going to have a conference here next spring.*
> *Are you going to visit the castle?*

- use *be* + *going to* + infinitive to describe personal plans and intentions for the future
- with the verb *go*, we usually say *be* + *going to*

1 **3.67** Complete the sentences from Listening exercise 1 with the *going to* form of the verbs in brackets. Then listen and check your answers.

1 We _____ the water park. (*visit*)
2 We _____ in them. (*swim*)
3 We _____ there. (*get married*)
4 We _____ a big party at a restaurant. (*have*)
5 We _____ some scenes in Malta. (*film*)
6 I _____ English there this summer. (*learn*)

2 Change these sentences so they are true for you.

- I'm not going to study English tonight.
- I'm going on a trip this weekend.
- I'm not going to see my family today.
- I'm going to have a holiday soon.
- I'm going to a restaurant this evening.

3 Work in pairs. Compare your sentences in exercise 2 and ask about your partner's plans and intentions.

A: *I'm not going to study English tonight.*
B: *No? What are you going to do?*
A: *I'm going to watch TV.*

Ⓖ **Grammar focus** – explanation & more practice of *going to* on page 150

Speaking

1 Work in pairs. These people are going to come to your city for a weekend. They want you to plan a weekend for them. Choose **one** of the groups of visitors.

A group of people with a lot of money
A group of people with not very much money
A family with small children
A group of people who love sports
A group of people who love culture

2 Prepare a list of things for them to do. Think about:

- accommodation (*they're going to stay at …*)
- food (*they're going to eat …*)
- things to do in the day (*they're going to visit …*)
- nightlife (*at night they're going to see …*)
- transport (*they're going to travel around the city by …*)

3 Tell another pair about your plans for the visitors.

They're going to stay in the Palace Hotel because they have a lot of money.

Vocabulary

1 Complete the verb phrases below with *-ing*, *-ball* or nothing (-).

basket____

foot____ (play) volley____

golf____ tennis____

swimm____ (go) ski____

cycl____ runn____

2 🔊 **3.68** Match the verb phrases in exercise 1 to the pictures. Then listen and check your answers. Say the verbs.

3 Work in pairs and ask each other the questions.

- Which sports do you like?
- Which sports do you do?
- Which sports do you watch on TV?

Reading

1 You are going to read about a special sports competition. Check you understand the words in the box.

| annual | homeless | objective |
| tournament | | |

2 🔊 **3.69** Read and listen to *A ball can change the world* on page 119. Find these numbers in the text. What do they mean in the text?

19
The number of countries in the first Homeless World Cup.

1 35   4 2003
2 73   5 100,000
3 144

3 Work in pairs. Ask and answer these questions.

- Are there many homeless people in your town or city?
- Are there projects to help them?
- Do you think the Homeless World Cup is a good idea? Can a ball *change the world*?

Extend your vocabulary — *-less, -ful*

We use the suffix *-less* to mean *without*, eg *homeless*

We use the suffix *-ful* to mean *with lots of*, eg *beautiful* (notice the spelling)

Some words can use both suffixes, eg *colourless, colourful*

Complete the sentences with the correct form of the words in brackets.

1 The injection I had was _____. It didn't hurt at all! *(pain)*
2 Be _____! That machine was very expensive. *(care)*
3 Our new cat is really _____. It loves being with the children. *(play)*
4 You need to check your work more. You've made some _____ mistakes. *(care)*
5 Oh what a _____ dress. Where did you buy it? *(beauty)*

a b c d e f g h i

Grammar

> *35%* **have found** *a job.*
> *The first Homeless World Cup* **was** *in Graz in 2003.*
>
> - use the present perfect when we don't know or say when the event happened
> - use the past simple when we say when the event happened and with time expressions such as *in 2007, four years ago, when I was 16, last week*

1 Circle the correct verb form.

The story of David Duke

Six years ago, David Duke *was / has been* homeless and he *didn't have / hasn't had* a job. He *has heard / heard* about the Homeless World Cup in 2004 and *has decided / decided* to join. He *has played / played* for Scotland in 2004. Since then, lots of good things *have happened / happened*. He *has gone / went* back to school. He *found / has found* a home. His team *has won / won* the Homeless World Cup in 2007.

2 Make questions with the present perfect.

1 you / ever / do / a sports class?
2 you / ever / do / any winter sports?
3 you / ever / see / an important sporting event live?
4 you / ever / play / a team sport?
5 you / ever / be / in a sporting competition?

G Grammar focus – explanation & more practice of the present perfect and past simple on page 150

Speaking

Work in pairs. Turn to page 133 and ask each other questions about sport.

A ball can change the world

> We're not all bad people. The only difference between us is that you have a home and we don't.
> **Dermot Haverty, Captain, Ireland**

There are one billion homeless people in our world today.

The Homeless World Cup is an annual, international football tournament. The objective is to end homelessness. The first Homeless World Cup was in the city of Graz, Austria in 2003. There were 19 countries. More than 144 homeless men and women played. Austria won the tournament.

The players say that the event changes their lives. For example, since the 2006 Homeless World Cup in Cape Town …

39% have gone back to school

35% have found a job

44% have found a home

92% of players have a new motivation for life

73% have changed their lives for the better

In addition, the organisers of the Homeless World Cup say that the event can change the way we see homeless people. More than 100,000 people watched the 2007 tournament in Copenhagen, Denmark.

> Playing in the Homeless World Cup has been a fantastic experience for all our team. We have all worked very hard and have learnt so much.
> **Ricardo Arma, Captain, Italy**

HOMELESS WORLD CUP

Pronunciation

1 🔊 **3.70** Listen and repeat the pairs of words. Can you hear the difference?

1	eat	it
2	car	call
3	met	meat
4	pig	big
5	open	opened
6	hi	eye
7	teen	ten
8	could	good
9	they	day
10	get	got

2 Choose six words from exercise 1 and put them in the grid below.

3 🔊 **3.71** Listen to the words. When you hear a word in your box, circle it. When you have marked all your words, call out *Bingo!*

Speaking and Reading

1 Work in pairs and discuss the questions.

- The pronunciation activity above was a game. Do you like playing games?
- Did you have a favourite game as a child? What was it? How do you play it?
- Have you played any other games that help you to learn English? Which games?

2 🔊 **3.72** Read and listen to *Kim's Game* on page 121. Have you heard of this game? How do you think people play it?

Listening

1 🔊 **3.73–3.75** Listen to people explaining three popular language games. Match the games 1–3 to the types of explanation a–c.

1 Categories
2 Kim's Game
3 Twenty Questions

a the description of the game
b a conversation about a game
c the instructions for the game

2 Choose one of the games. Listen again and make some notes about the rules.

3 Work in pairs. Explain the rules of the game, but use your own words.

Vocabulary

1 Complete the expressions with a word from the box. Use a dictionary to help you. There is one word you do not need.

cheating	game	lose	my	points
turn	wins			

1 Every time I play with him I _____. He's better than me.
2 It's _____ turn.
3 No _____! You can't look at the cards.
4 The objective is to get a hundred _____.
5 The person with the most points _____ the game.
6 Whose _____ is it?

2 🔊 **3.76** Listen and check your answers.

Speaking

1 Work in small groups. Choose one of the games from the listening or another game you know that helps you to learn English. Play the game.

2 When you finish, tell the class.

Kim's Game

Kim's Game originally comes from a book called *Kim* by the English writer Rudyard Kipling. In the book, the main character Kim plays this game to train his powers of observation and become a spy for the British government in India and Asia.

The game became very popular with the American Boy Scouts organisation and is also a popular game for language learners.

It's easy to play Kim's game …

Nobody really knows what the world's oldest game is. Some people say the Chinese board game of *Go* is the oldest in the world (more than 4,000 years old).

Rudyard Kipling (1865–1936) was the first English writer to receive the Nobel Prize for Literature. Kipling was born in Mumbai (formerly Bombay), and many of his books are about India. His most famous books are *The Jungle Book*, *Just So Stories* and *Kim*.

10 Function globally making suggestions

a   b   c   d

Warm up

Work in pairs. Look at the pictures and answer the questions.

1   Do you know any of these sights? What do you know about them?
2   Have you visited any of these sights?
3   Which sights would you like to see?
4   What other world famous sights can you think of?
5   What are the most famous sights in your country?

Listening

1   🔘 3.77–3.79 Listen to three conversations between tour guides and tourists. Match each one to a picture. There is one picture you do not need.

2   Listen again and answer the questions.

Conversation 1: Is it their first visit to Egypt?
            What time does the sight open?
Conversation 2: Where is the Kremlin?
            Are there long queues to see it?
Conversation 3: Has the woman visited Turkey before?
            What are they going to do first?

Language focus: making suggestions

1   🔘 3.80 Read and listen to how people make and respond to suggestions from the listening.

Asking for a suggestion	What do you suggest? What would you like to see?
Making suggestions	Let's see the pyramids. Why don't we go to your hotel first? We can go and see the sights.
Responding (affirmative)	Oh, yes. Good idea.
Responding (negative)	I don't know. Oh, no thanks.

2   Make suggestions with the prompts.

•   go to the cinema
•   go and have a coffee
•   get something to eat
•   take a taxi to class
•   walk home together
•   go shopping

3   Work in pairs. A: make a suggestion from the list above. B: respond. Then swap roles and repeat.

Speaking

Work in pairs and choose **one** of the tasks below.

A   Look at the audioscript on page 157 and choose one of the conversations. Change some details and practise it.

B   A: you are a visitor to B's country. B: you want to show the visitor some nice sights. Make suggestions. The visitor responds.

Unit 4, Speaking (page 47)

Look at the picture. What do you see? Describe your breakfast table to your partner and ask them questions about theirs. How many differences can you find?

A: *On my breakfast table I have … Do you?*
B: *Yes, I do. / No, I don't. And what about …?*
A: *I don't have any …*

Unit 7, Speaking (page 85)

1 Look at the table below and ask your partner questions to complete it.

A: *Where did you go?*
B: *I went …*

	Student A	Student B
where / go?	Music festival	
how / travel?	By train	
who / go with?	Three friends from work	
have / good time?	It was OK. Rained a lot	
do / there?	Saw lots of bands	

2 Answer your partner's questions about your day out.

Unit 9, Vocabulary and Speaking (page 102)

1 You and your partner both have a picture of a mountain scene and a park scene. The pictures are similar but there are some differences. Describe your mountain scene to your partner and answer their questions. Use the useful language below to help you.

Useful language

- There's a … / There are some …
- In the centre / On the right / On the left …
- In the distance …
- Is there a …? / Are there any …?
- What colour are …?
- How big is …?

2 Listen while your partner describes their park scene. What differences can you hear? Ask questions to check before you look at their picture.

Unit 9, Reading (page 104)

In El Salvador and other Central American countries, a girl has a party when she is 15 years old. It is called the *quinceañera*. They say it is the happiest time of a girl's life. It can also be the most expensive event for the girl's family. The girl's dress is an important part of the party. The most common colour is white or pink. In some *quinceañera* parties the girl starts with a white dress and then changes into a pink dress. After the party she is considered to be a woman.

1 Read the text and answer the questions in Reading exercise 2 on page 104.

2 Work in pairs and tell your partner about the rite of passage.

3 Do you have any special celebrations like these in your country?

Communication activities: Student B

Unit 1, Vocabulary (page 12)

1 Write down the email and website addresses your partner says.

2 Dictate these email and website addresses to your partner.

- jillpotter@yahoo.es
- xray.man@telemail.net
- www.dictionary.com/english

Unit 2, Grammar (page 21)

1 Read the text below about a created capital.

Canberra (capital from 1908) is the capital of Australia. It is in the south-east of the country, about 250 km from Sydney. The population of Canberra is small. It is only about 350,000. It's a modern city and it has nice weather.

2 Find out about your partner's city. Ask and answer the questions from Grammar exercise 1 on page 21.

Unit 2, Vocabulary and Listening (page 24)

1 Dictate these dates to your partner.

13th October   31st August   25th May   26th July

2 Write down the dates your partner says.

3 Check your answers together.

Unit 4, Speaking (page 43)

1 Work in small groups and create an unusual hotel. Use the ideas in the box, the pictures and the text on page 43 to help you. Make notes of where it is, the prices and the facilities.

in a school	on the beach	on a bus

2 Work with students from group A and exchange information. Find a hotel you like.

Unit 4, Speaking (page 47)

Look at the picture. What do you see? Describe your breakfast table to your partner and ask them questions about theirs. How many differences can you find?

B: *On my breakfast table I have … Do you?*
A: *Yes, I do. / No, I don't. And what about …?*
B: *I don't have any …*

Unit 7, Speaking (page 85)

1 Look at the table below and answer your partner's questions about your day out.

A: *Where did you go?*
B: *I went to my aunt's wedding.*

	Student A	**Student B**
where / go?		Aunt's wedding
how / travel?		By car
who / go with?		My family
have / good time?		It was great! Weather was fantastic
do / there?		Danced and ate

2 Ask your partner questions to complete the table.

Unit 9, Vocabulary and Speaking (page 102)

1 You and your partner both have a picture of a mountain scene and a park scene. The pictures are similar but there are some differences. Listen while your partner describes their mountain scene. What differences can you hear? Ask questions to check before you look at their picture. Use the useful language below to help you.

Useful language

- There's a … / There are some …
- In the centre / On the right / On the left …
- In the distance …
- Is there a …? / Are there any …?
- What colour are …?
- How big is …?

2 Describe your park scene to your partner and answer their questions.

Unit 9, Reading (page 104)

In Britain, Australia and New Zealand an important time for a young person is their 'coming of age'. In the past this was on their 21st birthday but now it is more common on their 18th birthday. The best thing about it is the party. The person usually invites their friends or family, and they bring more expensive gifts than usual. This is the time when a young person becomes an adult. They can vote or drink alcohol.

1 Read the text and answer the questions in Reading exercise 2 on page 104.

2 Work in pairs and tell your partner about the rite of passage.

3 Do you have any special celebrations like these in your country?

Additional material

Unit 8, Speaking (page 91)

1 Look at the questionnaire on transport. Choose four questions and ask and answer in pairs.

Q TRANSPORT

● Is traffic a problem in your town?

● Do you live near your work or far away?

● Is parking a problem in your town?

● Do you travel around the city by public transport or do you take the car?

● Is public transport cheap or expensive in your town?

● Do you prefer to go on foot or by bicycle?

● Are people using bicycles more in your town?

● On a long trip do you prefer to go by car or by train?

2 Work with a different partner. Close your books. Ask each other the questions again.

Do you live near your work or far away?
I live near my office.
Is parking a problem in your town?
Yes, it's expensive and it's difficult to find a space.

Unit 8, Writing (page 95)

1 Read two emails from someone living in a new country or city. Choose one of the emails and complete the sentences with your own ideas.

● ○ ○

Dear _____ (person)

It's my first week here in _____ (city or country). I love it! The people here are _____ (comparative adjective) than at home. We went to a _____ (place) last night and it was great.

That's all for now.

● ○ ○

Dear _____ (person)

Well, I'm still in _____ (city or country). Things aren't so good now. I don't have many friends and I'm feeling _____ (comparative adjective) than before. I didn't do anything last night.

That's all for now.

2 Continue the email. Use the sentences in Grammar exercise 2 on page 95 to help you.

3 Work in pairs and swap your emails.

Unit 10, Speaking (page 119)

1 Complete the middle column with questions from Grammar exercise 2 on page 119.

2 Work in pairs. Ask and answer the questions. If your partner says *Yes*, ask them the questions in the Yes box. If they say *No*, ask them the questions in the No box.

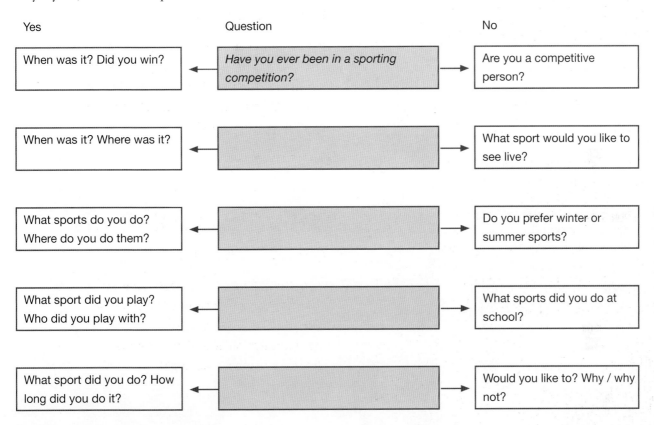

Yes	Question	No
When was it? Did you win?	*Have you ever been in a sporting competition?*	Are you a competitive person?
When was it? Where was it?		What sport would you like to see live?
What sports do you do? Where do you do them?		Do you prefer winter or summer sports?
What sport did you play? Who did you play with?		What sports did you do at school?
What sport did you do? How long did you do it?		Would you like to? Why / why not?

A: *Have you ever taken part in a sporting competition?*
B: *Yes, I was in an athletics competition.*
A: *When was it?*
B: *When I was at school.*
A: *Did you win?*
B: *No, I was third.*

Additional material

Phonetic symbols

Single vowels

/ɪ/	fish	/fɪʃ/	(build, busy, English, women)
/iː/	bean	/biːn/	(he, key, niece, people)
/ʊ/	foot	/fʊt/	(could, put, woman)
/uː/	shoe	/ʃuː/	(fruit, rule, through, two)
/e/	egg	/eg/	(breakfast, friend, many, said)
/ə/	mother	/mʌðə/	(arrive, colour, police)
/ɜː/	word	/wɜːd/	(learn, curly, skirt, birthday)
/ɔː/	talk	/tɔːk/	(four, horse, thought, water)
/æ/	back	/bæk/	(fat, cat, catch, bag)
/ʌ/	bus	/bʌs/	(blood, does, enough, onion)
/ɑː/	arm	/ɑːm/	(aunt, heart, laugh, past)
/ɒ/	top	/tɒp/	(what, stop, hot)

Diphthongs

/ɪə/	ear	/ɪə/	(here, Italian, theatre)
/eɪ/	face	/feɪs/	(break, eight, email, say, they)
/ʊə/	tourist	/tʊərɪst/	(plural, sure)
/ɔɪ/	boy	/bɔɪ/	(noise, toy)
/əʊ/	nose	/nəʊz/	(although, coat, know, no)
/eə/	hair	/heə/	(careful, their, wear, where)
/aɪ/	eye	/aɪ/	(five, buy, die, my)
/aʊ/	mouth	/maʊθ/	(town)

Consonants

/p/	pen	/pen/	(happy)
/b/	bag	/bæg/	(rabbit)
/t/	tea	/tiː/	(ate, fatter, worked)
/d/	dog	/dɒg/	(address, played)
/tʃ/	chip	/tʃɪp/	(natural, watch)
/dʒ/	jazz	/dʒæz/	(age, bridge, generous)
/k/	cake	/keɪk/	(chemistry, kitchen, toothache)
/g/	girl	/gɜːl/	(foggy, dog)
/f/	film	/fɪlm/	(different, laugh, photograph)
/v/	verb	/vɜːb/	(of, very)
/θ/	thing	/θɪŋ/	(thin, think)
/ð/	these	/ðiːz/	(that, those, mother)
/s/	snake	/sneɪk/	(city, message, race)
/z/	zoo	/zuː/	(has)
/ʃ/	shop	/ʃɒp/	(description, machine, sugar)
/ʒ/	television	/teləvɪʒən/	(garage, usual)
/m/	map	/mæp/	(summer)
/n/	name	/neɪm/	(sunny, knife)
/ŋ/	ring	/rɪŋ/	(sing, tongue)
/h/	house	/haʊs/	(who)
/l/	leg	/leg/	(hill, possible)
/r/	road	/rəʊd/	(carry, write)
/w/	wine	/waɪn/	(one, why)
/j/	yes	/jes/	(used)

Letters of the alphabet

/eɪ/	/iː/	/e/	/aɪ/	/əʊ/	/uː/	/ɑː/
Aa	Bb	Ff	Ii	Oo	Qq	Rr
Hh	Cc	Ll	Yy		Uu	
Jj	Dd	Mm			Ww	
Kk	Ee	Nn				
	Gg	Ss				
	Pp	Xx				
	Tt	Zz				
	Vv					

Unit 1

Articles (*a, an*)

Singular nouns

Use the indefinite article *a / an* with singular nouns.

Use *a* with singular nouns starting with a consonant sound.
*a computer, **a** video*

Use *an* with singular nouns starting with a vowel sound.
***an** apple, **an** umbrella*

Plural nouns

For plural nouns, write a number or no article.
***two** computers*
computers

Plural spelling

- for most nouns add *s* to form the plural: ***an** airport – airports*
- for nouns ending in consonant + *y*, delete *y* and add *ies*: *a family – families*
- for nouns ending in *ch*, *sh*, *s* and *x* add *es* to form the plural: *sandwich – sandwiches*

be

Affirmative (+)	Negative (-)	Question (?)	Short answer
I **am** (**I'm**) 35.	I **am not** (**I'm not**) Mr Norris.	**Am** I in this class?	**Yes**, I **am**. **No**, I'm **not**.
You / We / They **are** (**You're** / **We're** / **They're**) students.	You / We / They **are not** (**aren't**) in this hotel.	**Are** you / we / they teachers?	**Yes**, you / we / they **are**. **No**, you / we / they **aren't**.
He / She / It **is** (**He's** / **She's** / **It's**) from England.	He / She / It **is not** (**isn't**) a doctor.	**Is** he / she / it from Japan?	**Yes**, he / she / it **is**. **No**, he / she / it **isn't**.

Possession

Subject pronoun	Possessive adjective
I	my
you*	your*
he	his
she	her
it	its
we	our
they	their

* *you* is both singular and plural

Unit 1 Exercises

Articles (*a, an*)

1 Write the correct article. Then write the plural form.

a computer   two computers
1 bus
2 apple
3 email
4 dictionary

2 Complete the sentences with the correct form: a / an / -.

He's _a_ doctor.
1 I'm ___ accountant.
2 I'm married, with ___ two daughters.
3 We live in ___ interesting little village, near Berlin.
4 There's ___ big lake, where we sometimes swim.
5 There's ___ tourist information centre in the village.
6 You can get ___ tour bus to take you around, if you want.
7 In summer ___ visitors come and camp by the lake.
8 It's ___ lovely place to stay.

be

3 Complete the sentences with the correct form of *be*.

They _are_ from Russia.
1 We ___ hotel directors.
2 They ___ German number plates.
3 It ___ a computer.
4 I ___ 36.
5 She ___ a teacher.
6 You ___ students.

5 Answer these questions with short answers. Make them true for you.

Are you a nurse? *No I'm not.*
1 Are you happy in your English class?
2 Is your partner in class from your country?
3 Are your classmates nice?
4 Is your English teacher friendly?
5 Is your homework easy?
6 Is English spelling difficult?
7 Are you all happy with this coursebook?

4 Rewrite these sentences according to the symbol in brackets.

He isn't a doctor. (?)   *Is he a doctor?*
1 Are we in this hotel? (+)
2 It's from the US. (-)
3 Am I a doctor? (-)
4 They aren't directors. (?)
5 You're not 21! (+)
6 She's a student. (?)

Possession

6 Decide if these sentences are correct (✔) or incorrect (✘). Then correct the mistakes.

Is this your book? ✔
I name is Sarah. ✘
My name is Sarah.
1 Is that your hotel?
2 They phone number is 021 455 6784.
3 Her is a photography student.
4 Her name is Isabella.
5 Ours books are in the classroom.
6 She is a doctor and his name is Angelina.
7 We are Portuguese but we teacher is American.
8 They are in room 108.

7 Complete the sentences with the correct form.

(student) Can you tell me _your_ address?
1 (student) Excuse me, I think that's _____ pencil.
2 (teacher) Can I have _____ homework, please?
3 (teacher) Where's Max? Does anyone have _____ phone number?
4 (students) Could you give us _____ exam results, please?
5 (student) Can I borrow _____ rubber, Sara?
6 (teacher) Please spell _____ surname for me, Eva.
7 (student) Maria is not coming today. _____ car isn't working.

Unit 2

Prepositions of place

- use *from* to say your country or home town or to say the distance from another place.
  I'm from Canberra. It's 650km from Melbourne.
- use *near* to describe proximity.
  It's near Sydney.
- use *in* for countries or regions.
  It's in Australia. It's in New South Wales.

Wh- questions

- use *what* to ask about things.
  What's your address?
  32 King Street, Liverpool.
- use *where* to ask about places.
  Where's he from?
  Nigeria.
- use *how old* to ask about age.
  How old is she?
  21 or 22.

- use *why* to ask about reasons.
  Why are they here?
  To rent a car.
- use *when* to ask about time.
  When is your meeting?
  6.30.

With *be* the order is question word + *be* + subject + etc.

Present simple, affirmative and negative

Affirmative	Negative
I / You / We / They **get up**. He / She / It **gets up**.	I / You / We / They **don't get up**. He / She / It **doesn't get up**.

Use the present simple to talk about:
- habits and routines.
  *I **get up** at seven o'clock.*
- things that are always true.
  *October **has** 31 days.*

Spelling rules for the third person (*he, she, it*)

- after most verbs add *s*: *I get up – he gets up, we live – she lives*
- after verbs ending in *y*, delete *y* and add *ies*: *they study – she studies*
- after verbs ending in vowels, *ch*, *sh*, *s* and *x*, add *es*: *you finish – he finishes, they go – she goes*
- verbs such as *be* and *have* are irregular: *be – he is, have – she has*

Form the negative with auxiliary *don't* (*do not*) or *doesn't* (*does not*) + infinitive.
*I get up – I **don't get up***
*We live – We **don't live***
*He finishes – He **doesn't finish***

Unit 2 Exercises

Prepositions of place

1 Read the text and choose the correct answer.

My name's Aki and I'm *from / in* Kyoto. It is *in / near* Japan. Kyoto is 450km *from / in* the capital, Tokyo. Kyoto is *near / in* the city, Osaka. About 2.6 million people live *in / from* Osaka.

2 Write a few sentences about yourself. Use *in*, *from* and *near*. You can use the ideas to help you.

I live in a small town in the north of Latvia, about an hour from the capital, Riga. I live in a small flat near town, five minutes walk from the supermarket …

in	near / from
(small / big) house	river
flat	town centre
village	shops
town	workplace
south of the country	school / college / university
a (nice / modern) place (called …)	the train station
the countryside	a park

Wh- questions

3 Complete the questions with the correct *Wh-* question word. Then answer them.

How old	~~What~~	What	When	Where	Why

  What is your name? *My name is Alberto.*
1 _____ are you from?
2 _____ are you?
3 _____ is your English class?
4 _____ is your phone number?
5 _____ are you interested in English?

4 Put the words below in the correct order to make questions. Then match the questions 1–5 to the correct answers a–e.

1 hotel Where the is ?   a Bogotá.
2 old your car is How ?   b Two years old.
3 in Why you New York are ?   c Near the airport.
4 capital What of Columbia is the ? d For a business meeting.
5 Manchester to When the is train ? e In ten minutes.

Present simple, affirmative and negative

5 Write sentences with the correct form of the present simple.

get up at 7 o'clock (she +)
She gets up at 7 o'clock.
1 use a computer (he -)
2 repeat the exercise (they -)
3 have a car (she +)
4 write emails at work (we +)
5 go home at 6.30 (he +)
6 start class at 9.00 (you -)
7 do her homework (she +)
8 listen to the radio (I -)

6 Read the text and choose the correct answer.

I (1) *work / works* in an office and my friend (2) *work / works* in a restaurant. Our days are very different. I (3) *get up / gets up* at seven o'clock and I start work at nine o'clock, but she (4) *don't start / doesn't start* work until five o'clock so she (5) *get up / gets up* at 11.00. I have lunch at work but she (6) *haves / has* lunch at home. I (7) *finish / do finish* work at half past five and I get home about half past six. She (8) *finishes / finishs* work at 1.00am and she (9) *get / gets* home at 1.30am. I (10) *don't work / not work* at the weekend, but she (11) *work / works* on Saturday and Sunday. She (12) *doesn't works / doesn't work* on Monday.

Units 3 & 4

Possessive 's

Use *'s* to show possession with people.
My mother's car. Not: ~~The car of my mother~~

We usually use *of* and not *'s* before things and places.
*The door **of** the classroom. The president **of** the United States.*

For regular plural nouns, write *s'*.
My sisters' husbands. (= I have more than one married sister)

For irregular plural nouns write *'s*.
The children's teacher.

Yes / No questions

Question	Short answer
Do I / you / we / they **work?**	**Yes**, I / you / we / they **do**. **No**, I / you / we / they **don't**.
Does he / she / it **work?**	**Yes**, he / she / it **does**. **No**, he / she / it **doesn't**.

Form *yes / no* questions with the auxiliary *do / does*. The order is
Do / Does + subject + infinitive.

For *yes / no* short answers, the order is
Yes / No + subject + *does / doesn't*.
***Does** he live in London?* **Yes, he does.** / **No, he doesn't.**

Wh- questions

Question words (*What? Where? How old? Why? When?*) go at the start of the question.

The order is *Wh*-question + *do / does* + subject + infinitive.
***Where** do you live?*

For more on the auxiliary *do / does* and *Wh*- question words see Grammar focus Unit 2 on page 138.

Object pronouns

Subject pronoun	I	you	he	she	it	we	they
Object pronoun	me	you	him	her	it	us	them

Use object pronouns **after** the verb.
*English? I love **it**.*
*I don't like **them** very much.*

there is / there are

Use *there is* and *there are* to say something or someone exists.

Form the affirmative with *there is* + singular noun and *there are* + plural noun.
***There's** a pen on the table.* **There are** *eight people in my class.*

Form the negative with **there isn't a** ... / **there aren't any** ...
***There isn't a** phone in here.* **There aren't any** *restaurants here.*

Form the question with *is / are + there + a / any.*
Is there a *bank near here?* **Are there any** *dictionaries?*

Countable and uncountable nouns

Countable nouns have a singular and a plural form. Most plural countable nouns end in *s*.

Use *a / an*, a number or *some* before countable nouns.
***a** hotel, **two** hotels, **some** hotels*

Use *some* or no article before uncountable nouns.
*I have **fruit** for breakfast.* *I'd like **some fruit**.*

Some nouns can be countable and uncountable.
I love tea. (uncountable – tea in general)
Two teas please. (countable – two cups of tea)

Quantifiers

Affirmative

Countable
There are **lots of** shops.
There are **some** books.

Uncountable
It costs **a lot of** money.
There's **some** food.

Negative and questions

Countable
How many bananas are there?
There aren't **any** apples.
Are there **any** restaurants?
There aren't **many** oranges.

Uncountable
How much rice is there?
There isn't **any** juice.
Is there **any** milk?
There isn't **much** fruit.

Units 3 & 4 Exercises

Possessive 's

1 Correct these sentences.

The friend of my daughter   *My daughter's friend*

1 the teacher of my son
2 the book of her friend
3 the hotel of our friends
4 the wife of my brother
5 the cars of the men
6 the home of his cousins

Yes / No questions

2 Match questions 1-5 to answers a-e. Then write the answers so they are true for you.

1 Do you and your family live in a city?
2 Does your sister have any children?
3 Do you have a brother?
4 Do your parents know any English people?
5 Does your uncle live near you?

a Yes, he does.
b Yes, they do.
c Yes, we do.
d No, I don't.
e No, she doesn't.

Wh- questions

3 Write questions about the underlined information.

What does he do?   He's <u>a radiologist</u>.

1 _____ He works <u>in a hospital</u>.
2 _____ He sees his sister <u>at the weekend</u>.
3 _____ She lives <u>in Manchester</u>.
4 _____ She has <u>two</u> children.
5 _____ Her children are <u>six and four</u>.

Object pronouns

4 Replace the underlined words with the correct object pronoun.

I work with <u>John</u>.   *I work with him.*

1 We visit <u>our parents</u> every weekend.
2 I live near <u>my brother</u>.
3 I work with <u>Maria</u>.
4 They live near <u>my wife and I</u>.
5 I love <u>their dog</u>.
6 I usually go on holiday with <u>my cousins</u>.

there is / there are

5 Make 4 sentences using the prompts below about a hotel.

1 a gym (✘)
2 guided tours (✘)
3 meeting rooms (✔)
4 a restaurant (✔)

Countable and uncountable nouns

6 Write countable (*C*) or uncountable (*U*).

1 milk
2 egg
3 cheese
4 bread
5 cake
6 dollar
7 money
8 time

7 Write sentences about the information using *lots of* (+++), *some* (++), *not much / many* (+), *not any* (-).

apples + *There aren't many apples.*

1 coffee (-)
2 juice (+++)
3 jam (+)
4 potatoes (+++)
5 bananas (++)
6 rice (++)
7 oranges (-)
8 milk (+)

Quantifiers

8 Read the dialogue and choose the correct option.

A: Would you like (1) *some / any* coffee? Oh, I'm sorry, there isn't (2) *some / any* coffee.
B: No problem. Can I have (3) *some / any* tea?
A: Sure. Would you like something to eat?

B: Yes, please.
A: Let's see – there's (4) *not much / not many* food in the house. Ah good – there are (5) *some / many* biscuits.
B: Great – thanks.

Units 5 & 6

Frequency adverbs (*every day, once a week ...*)

To ask about frequency, use the question *How often ...?*

The order is *How often + do +* subject *+* verb.
How often *do you watch foreign films?*

We can give a specific answer with
every + day / week / month / year, etc.
*I go to the cinema **every week**.*

We can say the number of times we do something with
once / twice / three times / four times + a day / week / month / year, etc.

(once = one time; twice = two times)

The frequency adverb normally goes at the end of the sentence.
*I have my English class **twice a week**.*

Frequency adverbs (*always, often ...*)

To give a more general answer about frequency, use *always, often, sometimes, not often, never*.

With most verbs the order is subject + frequency adverb + verb.
*I **sometimes** watch TV on the internet.*

With *be* the order is subject + *be* + frequency adverb.
*She is **always** late.*

can

Use *can +* verb (without *to*) to talk about possibilities.
*We **can** use the company's sports club.*
Not: ~~*We can to use the company's sports club.*~~

Can does not change in the third person.
*I **can** use the company car.*
*My wife **can** use the company car too.*

To form the negative, add *not ('t)*.
*I **can't** walk to my office.*
*She **can't** eat for free.*

To form questions, the order is *Can +* subject + verb.
Can *you use the company car?*
Can *she make personal calls?*

Adverbs with *can*

Use *can / can't +* verb to describe abilities.
*I **can** type.   I **can't** speak German.*

Use adverbs to describe how we do things. We form most adverbs by adding *ly* to the adjective: *quick – quickly, bad – badly*
*He can type very **quickly**.   They speak English **badly**.*

If the adjective ends in *y*, we form the adverb with *ily*: noisy – nois**ily**

Some adverbs are irregular: *good – well, fast – fast*.
*She plays the piano **well**.   He can swim very **fast**.*

was / were

Affirmative	Negative	Question	Short answer
I / He / She / It **was.**	I / He / She / It **wasn't** (**was not**).	**Was** I / he / she / it?	**Yes**, I / he / she / it **was**. **No**, I / he / she / it **wasn't**.
You / We / They **were.**	You / We / They **weren't** (**were not**).	**Were** you / we / they?	**Yes**, you / we / they **were**. **No**, you / we / they **weren't**.

Was / were is the past form of the verb *be*.
*We **were** late for work today.*

Form the negative with *was + not (n't)*.
*I **wasn't** good at maths.*

Questions with *was / were*

For *yes / no* questions use *Was / Were +* subject.
Were *you a good student?*

For other questions the order is *Wh-* question word + *was / were +* subject. *Where **was** your school?*

Units 5 & 6 Exercises

Frequency adverbs (*every day, once a week ...*)

1 Put the words in the correct order to make questions.
Then answer them.

1 cinema do go you How to the often ?
2 often do the How you watch news ?
3 friends How see often you do your ?

4 have English often How your class do you ?
5 you documentaries often How do watch ?

Frequency adverbs (*always, often ...*)

2 Rewrite these sentences with the frequency adverb in the correct position.

1 I watch TV with my wife. (never)
2 The children are in front of the TV when I get home. (often)
3 He plays video games. (sometimes)
4 She is the first to get to the English class. (always)
5 They go on holiday abroad. (not often)
6 We go to bed early. (often)

3 Correct the sentences.

1 Never I watch TV in the mornings.
2 They go the cinema one a month.
3 She goes to the gym every weeks.
4 How often you go home for lunch?
5 I get up at 6.00am three time a week.
6 We not often play computer games.
7 He often is late for work.
8 I go to an exhibition two times a year.

can

4 Write sentences based on the information in the table.

You can swim.

	swim	speak Arabic	drive
you	✔	✘	?
he	?	✔	✘
they	✘	?	✔

5 Find and correct six mistakes in the dialogue.

A: Do you can use a computer?
B: Well, I can to do basic things: I'm can write documents and send emails but I can't do anything complicated. My brother's the expert. He works in computer graphics and he cans do programming.
A: Perhaps he can to help me with my computer.
B: I'll ask him.

Adverbs with *can*

6 Write positive and negative sentences with *can* using the prompts.

I / type / quick (✔) I can type quickly.
1 I / swim / quick (✔)
2 He / draw / good (✘)
3 They / play the piano / good (✔)

4 You / Speak English / good (✘)
5 She / speak / quiet (✘)
6 She / learn new things / easy (✔)

was / were

7 Complete the sentences with *was, were, wasn't* or *weren't*.

Last week my family and I (1) _____ in Morocco on holiday. We (2) _____ in Marrakesh. We (3) _____ happy with the hotel – it was dirty! And the weather (4) _____ good – it rained every day! But the people (5) _____ friendly and the food (6) _____ delicious.

8 Complete the questions with *Was* or *Were*. Then match the questions to the answers.

1 _____ you late for work?
2 _____ the film scary?
3 _____ your mother at home?
4 _____ we in the newspaper?
5 _____ your parents on holiday?
6 _____ your brother at work?

a No, they weren't.
b No, he wasn't.
c No, it wasn't.
d Yes, I was.
e Yes, she was.
f Yes, we were.

Unit 7

Past simple (regular verbs)

Use the past simple to talk about completed actions in the past, usually at a specific time.

The time expressions *yesterday*, *last week / month / year* and *five years ago* are often used with the past simple.

I watched a good film yesterday.

-ed spelling

- for most verbs add *ed*: answ**er** – answer**ed**
- for verbs ending in *e*, add *d*: creat**e** – creat**ed**
- for verbs ending in *y*, change the *y* to *ied:* tr**y** – tr**ied**. (But verbs ending in vowel + *y* are regular: pl**ay** – play**ed**).
- for verbs ending in consonant-vowel-consonant, double the consonant and add *ed*: sto**p** – stop**ped**

Use the same form for all persons (*I, you, he, she, it, we, they*) except for the verb *to be*.

Past simple (irregular verbs)

Many common verbs have an irregular affirmative form.

Infinitive	Past Simple
be	was / were
become	became
begin	began
buy	bought
can	could
come	came
choose	chose
do	did
drink	drank
drive	drove
eat	ate
feel	felt
get	got
go	went
have	had

Infinitive	Past Simple
hear	heard
know	knew
learn	learnt
leave	left
make	made
meet	met
ride	rode
run	ran
see	saw
sing	sang
sit	sat
sleep	slept
swim	swam
take	took
think	thought
win	won
write	wrote

it

Use *it* to:
- replace singular nouns.
  *Where's my book? I saw **it** in the kitchen.*
- talk about the time, the weather, the date, etc.
  ***It's** six o'clock. **It's** the 7th July today.*

Don't repeat *it* when you have another subject.
My car is blue.
Not: ~~My car it's blue.~~

Past simple (questions and negative)

Affirmative	Negative	Question	Short answer
I / You / He/ She / It / We / They **answered** the phone.	I / You / He/ She / It / We / They **did not** (**didn't**) **answer** the phone.	**Did** I / you / he / she / it / we / they **answer** the phone?	**Yes**, I / you / he / she / it / we / they **did**. **No**, I / you / he / she / it / we / they **didn't**.

Form past simple questions and negatives with the auxiliary verb *did*.
***Did** you enjoy the party?*
*They **didn't** go to the museum.*

With *Wh-* questions the order is
Wh- question word + *did* + subject + verb.
***Where did** you **go** last night?*

Unit 7 Exercises

Past simple (regular verbs)

1 Write the past simple form of these regular verbs.

1 talk
2 ask
3 stop
4 use
5 print
6 like
7 want
8 chat
9 start
10 study

2 Use these verbs to complete the description. Change them to the correct past form.

cook	start	arrive	want	visit	study	phone	finish
talk	show						

I was very busy yesterday evening. When I (1) _____ home, I (2) _____ my grandmother because it was her birthday. It was sunny so I (3) _____ English for an hour in my garden. Then a friend (4) _____ because she (5) _____ to see my new house, so I (6) _____ her around. We (7) _____ for a couple of hours, and I (8) _____ dinner. After eating, we (9) _____ listening to music. When we (10) _____, it was after 1.00am! It was fun, but I am very tired today!

Past simple (irregular verbs)

3 Complete the text with the correct past simple form of the verb in brackets. Some verbs are regular and some are irregular.

Katharine Graham _____ (be) born in 1917. She _____ (go) to Chicago university and later _____ (work) at *The Washington Post* as a journalist. She _____ (become) the publisher of *The Washington Post* in 1963 following the time of the Watergate scandal, a story that _____ (end) Nixon's presidency. She later _____ (write) her autobiography, *Personal History*. The book _____ (win) the Pulitzer Prize in 1998. She _____ (die) in 2001.

4 Write full answers to the questions about yourself.

What did you have for breakfast this morning? *I had some fruit and yoghurt.*

1 What time did you leave home this morning?
2 How did you get to school / work / college?
3 Did you have any problems on the way?
4 Who did you speak to this morning before 10.30 am?
5 Did you do any work last night?
6 What did you have for your evening meal?
7 Did you make it yourself?
8 What time did you go to bed?
9 How did you sleep?

it

5 Decide if these sentences are correct (✔) or incorrect (✗). Then correct the mistakes.

1 It's 10 o'clock.
2 My birthday it's in June.
3 Is warm and sunny today.
4 Is that fish? I'm afraid I can't eat it.
5 What time is?
6 I like this book. Is about a family in the 1920s.

6 Write what you think 'it' refers to in these sentences.

It's very sunny today. *The weather*

1 It's fantastic, and a lovely colour too. I get to work really quickly now!
2 I don't really know, but it's probably about 2.30.
3 It's beautiful! Is it a boy or a girl?
4 My teacher gave me this, but it's really difficult and I can't do it.
5 It's sweet and people eat it for breakfast on bread.
6 I love it. I can wear it for my cousin's wedding.
7 Don't sit on it. It's still wet!
8 Can I have a piece? It looks and smells delicious!

Past simple (questions and negative)

7 Change the sentence according to the symbol in brackets.

I didn't answer the phone. (?)
Did you answer the phone?

1 I walked to the musuem. (-)
2 Did you know her name? (-)
3 They didn't get up early. (?)
4 She left when the class finished. (?)
5 He didn't write her an email. (+)
6 Did they go to the meeting? (+)
7 I didn't ask the teacher. (?)
8 I saw him at the office. (-)

8 Write questions for the answers about a holiday.

Who did you go with? I went with my husband.

1 _____? We went to Lisbon.
2 _____? We went last summer.
3 _____? We stayed in a hotel.
4 _____? We went to museums, we visited the old town and we went to the coast for a day.
5 _____? We were there for a week.
6 _____? We ate fish and seafood.

Audioscript

Unit 1

🔘 1.13

a eleven, twelve, thirteen, fourteen, fifteen …

b four, six, eight …

c seventh, eighth, ninth …

d ninety-nine, ninety-six, ninety-three …

🔘 1.14

a eleven, twelve, thirteen, fourteen, fifteen, sixteen, seventeen …

b four, six, eight, ten, twelve …

c seventh, eighth, ninth, tenth, eleventh …

d ninety-nine, ninety-six, ninety-three, ninety, eighty-seven …

🔘 1.17

1 **A:** Good morning, sir.
  B: Morning. My name's Steinbeck.
  A: Ah yes, Mr and Mrs Steinbeck. Two nights.
  B: That's right.
  A: Thank you. And your phone number please?
  B: Sorry?
  A: What's your telephone number?
  B: Ah, 00 44 1845 705 881
  A: And finally your email address, please.
  B: peter.steinbeck@blc.net
  A: Thank you Mr Steinbeck. Joe?
  C: Yes?
  A: Please show Mr and Mrs Steinbeck their room. Here's their key. Room 224.
  C: No problem.
  B: Thank you.

🔘 1.18

2 **A:** Excuse me. It's my wife. She needs to see a doctor.
  B: Name?
  A: Sorry?
  B: What's her name?
  A: Morley. Lisa Morley. It's rather urgent.
  B: Can you spell that please?
  A: Yes, M-O-R-L-E-Y. Can she see a doctor?
  B: What's your phone number Mr Morley?
  A: 01202 67110.
  B: Can you repeat that please?
  A: Oh for goodness … 01202 67110.
  B: And your address?
  A: What? Oh … er … 15 Bedford Road, Bedford. B-E-D-F-O-R D. Now can she see a doctor? She's having a baby!

🔘 1.20

1 **A:** Mike, hi.
  B: Hey Lauren, how's it going?
  A: Fine thanks. Good to see you.
  B: Yeah. Sit down.
  A: Thanks.
  B: Coffee?
  A: Yes, please.

🔘 1.21

2 **A:** Doctor Sim, hello.
  B: Hello Doctor James.
  A: This is Doctor Hathaway. She's new here. It's her first day.
  C: Hello.
  B: Pleased to meet you Doctor Hathaway.
  C: Nice to meet you.

🔘 1.22

3 **A:** Taxi!
  B: Kate?
  A: Yes?
  B: Kate! How are you?
  A: I'm OK, thanks. Um …
  B: I'm Rob! From school? Remember me?
  A: Ah. Yes. How are you?
  B: Fine. Fine. Kate. Kate Greenfield. It is you?
  A: Er … Yes. Listen, this is my taxi.
  B: It's good to see you.
  A: Good to see you too Rob but I …
  B: Wow. Kate Greenfield.

🔘 1.23

4 **A:** Excuse me, are you Mr Brown?
  B: No, I'm not.
  A: Sorry. Excuse me, Mr Brown?
  C: What?
  A: Are you Mr Brown?
  C: No, I'm not.
  A: Sorry!
  D: Excuse me. My name's Frank Brown, and I'm …
  A: You're Mr Brown!
  D: Yes, I am.
  A: Mr Brown, my name's David Jones from ING Electrics.
  D: Oh, hello. Nice to meet you.
  A: Nice to meet you too. Welcome to London. How are you?
  D: I'm fine, thank you. A bit tired.

🔘 1.24

1 My name is Aki Makino and I'm from Tokyo.

🔘 1.25

2 My name is Menahi. I'm from Saudi Arabia.

🔘 1.26

3 My name is Kristina. I come from Russia.

🔘 1.27

4 My name is Hani Al Quhayz. I am from Saudi Arabia, I am from Riyadh. Riyadh is the capital of Saudi Arabia.

🔘 1.28

5 So, my name is Elodie. I come from Switzerland, from Geneva.

🔘 1.29

6 My name is Liliya. I come from the Ukraine.

🔘 1.30

7 My name is Sara Catozzi, I live in Rome.

🔘 1.31

8 I am Maxim. I am from Russia. I am from Moscow.

🔘 1.32

9 I'm Elizabeth. I'm from Germany.

🔘 1.33

10 My name's Amy. I'm from China.

Unit 2

🔘 1.37

1 **A:** Well, see you later then.
  B & C: OK, bye.
  B: Your boyfriend's nice. Where's he from?
  C: Moscow.
  B: Oh. Is he Russian?
  C: No, he isn't Russian. He lives in Scotland.
  B: Scotland?
  C: Yes, he's from Moscow, Scotland.
  B: Moscow, Scotland? Where's that?
  C: It's a small place 50 kilometres from Glasgow.
  B: Well, I never.

🔘 1.38

2 **A:** Good morning.
  B & C: Hello.
  A: Your names please?
  B: I'm Louise Maloney and this is my husband, Scott. We have a reservation.
  A: OK. Can I have some personal details please? Can you spell your surname please?
  B: Of course. That's M-A-L-O-N-E-Y.
  A: Thank you. Where are you from Mrs Maloney?
  B: We're from Paris.
  A: Paris, France.
  C: Oh no, we're not French.
  A: But you're from Paris!
  C: Yes, we are. We're from Paris, Texas in the US. It's near Dallas.
  A: Oh, I see. I'm sorry. Paris, Texas, US.

🔘 1.39

3 **A:** Next. Name?
  B: I'm sorry?
  A: What's your name?
  B: Miguel Hernández.
  A: Where are you from Mr Hernández?
  B: Madrid.
  A: Passport?
  B: Sorry, I don't …
  A: Can I see your passport please?
  B: Oh OK, here you are.
  A: But this is a Mexican passport. Are you Mexican?
  B: Yes, I am.
  A: But you come from Madrid.
  B: Yes, that's right. Not Madrid in Spain, Madrid in Mexico.

1.43

1 A: Hello, I have a meeting with Mrs Bristow, the Commercial Director at 4.15.
   B: Your name please?
   A: Stuart Barnes from LDT Communications.
   B: One moment please. Mrs Bristow? Mr Barnes is here to see you.

 1.44

2 A: OK let's see … The London train goes from platform four at 3.20. What's the time now?
   B: It's only 2.45. Would you like to have a coffee before you go? Look, there's a café over there.
   A: Yeah good idea. The coffee on trains is always terrible.

 1.45

3 A: Do you want to go to the cinema on Friday?
   B: Yes OK. What time's the film?
   A: It's on at 6.00.
   B: Oh, I go to the gym at 6.00.
   A: OK, what about 8.30?
   B: Yes, that's fine.

1.46

Well, my Spanish day is different from my English day. First of all, in Spain I get up at about 8.00 in the morning, a bit later than in England. And lunch … well in England I eat at 12:30, but in Barcelona that's very early, I normally eat at about 2.00. We have dinner later in Spain. A normal time to have dinner at home is 9.00. Finally, I go to bed at a different time when I'm in Barcelona. Normally about midnight. Yeah, I normally go to bed at 12.00 in Spain.

1.54

1 A: Excuse me? Um … hello? Excuse me?
   B: Yes?
   A: Yes. Hello. When is the next bus to the airport?
   B: To where?
   A: To the airport.
   B: …
   A: What? Excuse me? What?
   B: A quarter past five.
   A: Five fifteen. Thank you.

1.55

2 A: Excuse me?
   B: Yeah?
   A: This bus goes to the city centre, right?
   B: Yep.
   A: What time?
   B: Two fifty.
   A: Two fifteen?
   B: No, two fifty. Ten to three.
   A: Great, thanks.
   B: You're welcome.

1.56

3 A: The 10.30 to Hamilton is now at bay 6. The 10.45 to Ottawa is now at bay 8. The 11.10 to London is now at bay 9. The 11.15 to New York is now at bay 11.
   B: What time is it?
   C: Ten thirty.
   B: Um, half past ten. Is there time to have a coffee?
   C: Our bus is in fifteen minutes. Yeah, I think so.
   B: OK.

Unit 3

1.60

1 It's yellow and black.
2 It's green, blue and black.
3 It's red, green and blue with a white line.
4 It's green, blue and black with a thin red line.

1.62

1 A: What's your name?
   B: Hilary Thomson.
   A: Where are you from Hilary?
   B: I'm from Edinburgh.
   A: And do you live in Edinburgh now?
   B: No, I live in Madrid in Spain.
   A: Do you have a family clan?
   B: Yes, we're part of the Campbell clan.
   A: The Campbells … OK, do you have a clan tartan?
   B: Yes, it's green, blue and black with a thin red line.
   A: And do you wear a kilt on special occasions?
   B: Well no, personally I don't. I think it's more typical for men to wear kilts. My father and brother wear kilts for weddings, New Year and maybe even for international football matches.
   A: Do you think clans are important to Scottish people now?
   B: Well, yes, I think they're important. For me it's something special about being Scottish.

1.63

2 A: What's your name?
   B: Gordon Liddle.
   A: And where are you from?
   B: Glasgow.
   A: Do you live there now?
   B: No, I live near Dundee and work at Dundee University.
   A: Do you have a family clan?
   B: No, I don't.
   A: So do you wear a kilt on special occasions?
   B: Yes, I do. I wear a kilt for weddings and for special dinners and parties.
   A: Do you think clans are important to Scottish people now?
   B: No, I don't. I think it's important for people in the US and Australia with Scottish family, but I don't think it's important for most Scottish people.

1.67

1 Ugh, dogs? I really hate them. They're awful animals.
2 We have a dog. Jupiter. He's sixteen years old, he's intelligent, friendly and we love him.
3 I like dogs. I like all animals, except cats. I don't like cats. They're very unfriendly.
4 My sister loves dogs. Her dog's name is Rufus. Personally, I don't like him very much. He's dirty and really stupid too.
5 I love my dog. Her name is Princess. She's beautiful. The problem is … she doesn't like me very much.
6 We live in a really small house, and we don't have cats or dogs. We would like a dog. We love them. But we don't have space.

1.69

1 A: Is this your first visit to Scotland?
   B: Yes, it is. I'm from Romania.
   A: Romania? What part of Romania?
   B: I'm from a small town near the capital.
   A: Really? My cousin works in Budapest.
   B: Budapest is in Hungary, not Romania.
   A: Oh. Sorry.
   B: It's OK. I live near Bucharest, not Budapest.
   A: OK.

1.70

2 A: Hello.
   B: Hi Jane! Is this little Michael?
   A: Yes, isn't he big now!
   B: He is! How old is he?
   A: He's two.
   B: Two? When's his birthday?
   A: In July.

1.71

3 A: So, what's Alan like?
   B: Oh, he's very nice, and intelligent.
   A: So?
   B: Well, he still lives with his parents.
   A: His parents? How old is he?
   B: Thirty-eight.
   A: Oh.

1.72

4 A: How's the new job?
   B: I like it.
   A: What time do you start?
   B: Early. Seven o'clock in the morning.
   A: Seven o'clock? Why do you start so early?
   B: Because I finish work at half past three.
   A: Oh.

1.73

Nicole, Switzerland
I come from a small family. I just have one brother.

Audioscript

1.74
Carmen, Spain
I am from a big family. Well I think it is a big family nowadays because we are five members in the family. I have one sister and one brother and my brother is older than me and my sister is younger than me. So I am in the middle.

1.75
Martin, Czech Republic
My mother, she has two sisters so I have lots of cousins and uncles, other relations.

1.76
Dot, Scotland
I'm from a small family. I have one brother.

1.77
Bea, England
I'm from quite a big family … I've got one sister but I've got lots and lots of cousins.

1.78
Ena, Bosnia
My family is very small. I don't have lots of people in my family. I have one brother. His name is Ismar.

Unit 4

2.07
A: Hi. So you're Beth, right?
B: Yup.
A: Hi, I'm Clare. Welcome!
B: Thanks!
A: Is it your first time in San Francisco?
B: Yes, it is.
A: OK, let me show you round. So, this is the kitchen …
B: Nice cooker! I love cooking.
A: Great, we really like cooking too. There are two bathrooms. This one has a shower and the one at the end has a bath.
B: OK.
A: Our bedroom is here and this is the living room! You'll be OK sleeping on the sofa?
B: Yeah fine. Well this is CouchSurfing!
A: Right. OK, well there's a lamp down there by the sofa.
B: OK, that's great. Now I'd really like to cook you guys a meal or something …

2.09
1 Kedgeree is an English-Indian dish. It's made of rice and sometimes includes fish and eggs.
2 Maple syrup is a type of liquid made from the sweet juice of the maple tree. Originally made by Native Americans, it is now a typical part of breakfast in Canada and the US. People usually have it with pancakes, a kind of flat cake.
3 Ackee is a kind of special fruit from Jamaica. It's red on the outside, and yellow with big black seeds on the inside. A traditional Jamaican breakfast has ackee and a kind of fish, called saltfish.

4 A beskuit or rusks is a kind of biscuit from South Africa. It's hard and dry, and people often eat it with a cup of tea.

2.13
1 A: Good afternoon. Welcome to the Holiday Hotel.
   B: Hello. Do you have any single rooms?
   A: Just a minute … Yes we do. Would you like a smoking or a non-smoking room?
   B: I'd like a non-smoking room please. I don't smoke.
   A: OK. Sign here please.
   B: Thank you.

2.14
2 A: Ah. Mr Phelps. Welcome to Chicago. Is this your first visit?
   B: Yes, it is.
   A: Please sit down. Would you like a coffee?
   B: No, thank you.
   A: Are you sure? We have a very good coffee machine.
   B: Thank you very much, but I'm fine.
   A: OK then. Would you like to meet my colleagues?
   B: Yes, please. That would be great.

2.15
3 A: Hello.
   B: Hi. Come in, come in. How are you?
   A: Fine, thanks. Here, this is for you.
   B: What a lovely plant! Thank you.
   A: You're welcome.
   B: Please, have a seat in the living room. Would you like something to drink?
   A: Yes, please. What do you have?
   B: Well, there's …

Unit 5

2.18
OK, if you look at the chart here, you'll see it's about world film production. Every year, the average number of films in the world is 3,975. Yes, 3,975 new films are made every year. The majority of these films are not from Hollywood, the United States or North America. They are from Asia. Asia makes 67% of the world's films. North America in fact only produces 10% of world films every year. And Europe produces 17% of world films every year which is more films than South America (only 3.5%) and Africa (2.5%), but also more than North America. As you can see, world cinema is not only Hollywood, it's much more.

2.24
1 No, I never watch comedy programmes. They're just not funny. I hate comedy. I don't often watch TV anyway.

2.25
2 Ooh yes, what I really like are horror films and, um, those, er, thrillers. I watch films in bed because they're always on late and we have a TV in the bedroom.

2.26
3 No, I don't often watch the news. I don't like it and anyway my husband is always home before me and … um … he just … he really only watches sport.

2.27
4 Yes, I do. I really like those documentaries about animals – the photography is fantastic. Oh and I sometimes watch documentaries about history too – yeah, I like them.

2.28
5 Mm, I don't watch a lot of sport, but I like tennis. Oh and I sometimes watch football with people from work. Oh and the Olympics – I love the Olympics.

2.34
1 A: Good afternoon.
   B: Yes, hello.
   A: Can I help you?
   B: Yes, please. How much does this DVD player cost?
   A: Just a minute. It's £69.
   B: OK, I'll take it.

2.35
2 C: Can I help you?
   B: Yes, where are the … um … horror films?
   C: Horror films? Old or new ones?
   B: The old horror films, please. Classic old films.
   C: Over there, next to the world cinema section.
   B: Thanks very much. Can I pay by credit card?
   C: Yes.

2.36
3 B: Excuse me? Where's the popcorn?
   D: There isn't any popcorn. We have crisps.
   B: OK. Four bags of crisps then. And these soft drinks please.
   D: That's £6.80. Would you like a bag?
   B: Yes, please.
   D: Here you are.

2.37
B: Hello? Hello? I have everything!
E: Hi.
B: OK, look … a new DVD player, some horror films and some crisps and drinks. Everything is ready. What's the matter?
E: The television … It's broken.

2.39
Leslie, Switzerland
I don't go to the cinema that often. Maybe once a month or it depends a little on the season because sometimes in winter there are many good films and … yeah … but I don't go to the cinema regularly.

2.40

Ryusuke, Japan

To improve my English I go to cinema in Oxford maybe twice a month.

2.41

Berangere, France

Like several times a month. Yeah, like maybe, yeah, two or three times a month.

2.42

Key, Hong Kong

Maybe once a month. It depends whether they have some good movies on show, yeah, but mainly we watch some western movies.

2.43

Gloria, Ghana

Once every two months. Not really.

2.44

Mireille, US

I sometimes go to the cinema. I go probably once a month, once every two months and it depends, on what movie I see. I sometimes go and see action, I sometimes see comedies.

Unit 6

2.46

1   I work in a primary school with eight-year-olds. The best thing about this job is working with children. You can make a real difference to their lives. Oh, and the holidays are good too. The worst thing? Some of the parents!

2.47

2   I work for a telephone company in a big office. The best thing is the people I work with – they're really nice. And I have a company car. But my boss is very strict – we can't make personal phone calls or use email.

2.48

3   I work in a laboratory for an international company. The best thing about my job is the money! The good salary means I can buy things I want. And I have a great pension plan. The bad part? The hours. I often work 10 hours a day.

2.49

4   I work for a sports club in the city centre. I like my job but the pay isn't really very good. The best thing about my job is the extras. I have free car-parking, I can use all the sports facilities and we get free lunches in the club's restaurant.

2.55

The first … library

The Great Library of Alexandria was the first, or one of the first, libraries in the world. It was founded in Alexandria, Egypt in the 3rd century BC. There weren't any books in the library in the beginning; the information was on long pieces of paper, called scrolls.

2.56

The first … distance learning programme

The University of London is an important institution in the United Kingdom. It was the first university with a distance learning programme. The programme started in 1858. The university now has a global community of students in 180 countries.

2.59

1   A: Right, can we finish quickly please?
     B: Yes, yes, I agree.
     C: I'm sorry, but we have a lot of things to talk about.
     A: It's a quarter to one. It's time for lunch soon.
     B: I'd like to go at one o'clock please. I need to send some important emails.
     C: OK, OK, the first thing is the annual sales figures. Now, we need to look at these very carefully.

2.60

2   A: Ah, good, you're here.
     B: Yes, you wanted to see me?
     A: Yes, could you close the door?
     B: OK, sure.
     A: Do you know why you're here?
     B: Er … no. Is everything fine with my work?
     A: Yes.
     B: I don't understand then.
     A: Good news. You have a new job. Would you like to be senior manager?
     B: Wow. Yes, I would! Senior manager. That's … that's great!
     A: Well done.

2.61

3   A: Can you take a photo of us?
     B: Oh, yes. Of course.
     A: OK, OK everyone! It's photo time. Everyone look at the camera please! Can you all look at the camera please?
     B: Say cheese.
     C: Cheese!
     D: I'd like a copy of that photo.
     E: Can I have a copy too please?
     A: OK, OK.

2.63

Matteo, Italy

I think my favourite teacher in high school in Italy was my … my ancient Greek teacher.

2.64

Eva, Switzerland

A teacher I remember from school was my German teacher. She was a teacher who was very interested in young people and was really interested in hearing what young people think, young people's opinions and it was very interesting.

2.65

Carmen, Spain

My favourite teacher was a woman that I have when I was fifteen years old. She was my mathematics teacher. She was really good. She explained everything really good and mathematics was easy for me with her.

2.66

Christina, Germany

I had a very good teacher in history class. His lessons were inspiring. It was my favourite class.

2.67

Bea, England

My favourite teacher at school was my primary school teacher when I was eight years old. His name was Mr Etherington.

Unit 7

3.01

In 1851 Paul Reuter, who later started Reuters press agency, used the telegraph to send news for the first time.

In 1920 Station 8MK in Detroit presented the first radio news programme.

The BBC World Service – originally called the BBC Empire Service – started in 1932 and in 1938 it started its first foreign language service in Arabic.

In 1962 AT&T launched Telstar into orbit. It was the first active communications satellite.

In 1969 more than 600 million people watched Neil Armstrong – the first man on the moon.

In 1980 the Columbus Dispatch in Ohio, US was the first newspaper to start a digital edition on the internet.

In the last part of the 20th century it was possible to watch news all day. In 1980 Ted Turner created the Cable News Network (CNN) – the first TV station to broadcast news 24 hours, 7 days a week. In 1996 the first 24-hour news station in Arabic, Al Jazeera, started in Doha, Qatar.

3.11

1   A: Good morning, Daily Post Newspaper. Claudia speaking.
     B: Hello, is the reporter Daniella Hammond there?
     A: No, I'm sorry she's out. Can I take a message?
     B: No, thank you. I'll call back.
     A: OK then. Goodbye.

3.12

2   A: Good morning, Daily Post Newspaper. Claudia speaking.
     B: Good morning. Can I speak to Daniella Hammond please?
     A: Certainly sir. Who's calling?
     B: A friend. I have some information for her.
     A: Just one moment please … I'm sorry. Miss Hammond is busy just now. Can she call you later?
     B: I'll wait.
     A: OK, hold please.

Audioscript

3.13

3 **A:** Hello?
   B: Hello. Is that Daniella Hammond?
   A: Yes, it is.
   B: Are you the Daily Post reporter, Daniella Hammond?
   A: Yes. Who's calling, please?
   B: I have some information for you. Very important information.
   A: Just a second, I'll get a pen.
   B: No! I can't talk now. Meet me by the phone box at Sunshine Square tonight. Half past eight.
   A: But …
   B: Be there.

3.14

4 **A:** Hello? Hello?
   B: Hello …
   A: I can't hear you. There's a storm …
   B: The information … very important … photos …
   A: Sorry? What?
   B: Look … in the trees. There's an envelope. In the envelope are some photos.
   A: What? What is in the photos?
   B: They show … they show …

3.16

Haruna, Japan
I think as almost all of the people I love sunny days, I love sunny weather because if … uh … if it rains, or if it's cloudy or like windy, or snowy, I don't want to go out.

3.17

Maida, Switzerland
I like it when it's sunny before all. I obviously prefer when it's warm and not too cold.

3.18

Al-Mutasem, Saudi Arabia
Um … well the weather in … uh … in Jeddah is … uh … always hot and … uh… has a lot of humidity.

3.19

Mireille, US
Um, let's see … I love … I like sunny weather but I don't like it when it is too hot. Um, I like it sunny and cool … um … and so I like the English weather for that. In California I like it when it's sunny also but not too hot, but sunny and warm enough to go to the beach.

Unit 8

3.26

A: This week I'm in Hong Kong to see a very unusual form of public transport: the Mid-Levels Escalator system. I'm standing at the top of about 800 metres of escalators, and it's absolutely impossible to see the bottom from here. Every day thousands of people use these escalators to go to work. It's 8am here in Hong Kong and right now the escalators are going down, but at ten o'clock

they change direction. As I'm standing here, literally hundreds of people are coming in at the entrance and onto the steps … Excuse me?
B: Yes?
A: Do you use the escalators every day?
B: Yes, that's right; I use them to go down to my office in the morning and then I come back at about 7pm on my way home.
A: And what do you think of the escalators?
B: Oh they're great. They save me about an hour.

3.32

1 Hi, yes it's me. Listen I'm at the airport. No, fine, fine. But my bags aren't here. I know, and I have a meeting in 30 minutes!

3.33

2 **A:** Well, this is goodbye.
   B: Yes. Goodbye.
   A: I … I love you. Call me.
   B: I promise. Goodbye. Goodbye.

3.34

3 **A:** Bruce?
   B: Jerry?
   A: Bruce! It is you! Wow! Great. Great to see you man!
   B: Aw, great to see you too!

3.35

4 **A:** What time is it now?
   B: It's ten past six.
   A: What time is our plane?
   B: Twelve thirty. Another six hours and twenty minutes to wait.

3.36

5 No, he isn't here. Did he say he was on the ten o'clock flight from Dublin? He did. But he isn't here. I don't know what to do. I just don't know what to do!

3.41

A: So, the map says there's a subway station near here.
B: Can we just ask someone?
A: No, no. I think I know … If we're here…
B: Excuse me!
C: Yes?
B: Is there a subway near here? We want to go to the British Museum.
C: You mean the Tube? Er … yes. You … er … go straight on. Then turn right. The underground is there. Take the Central line for the British Museum.
B: Thank you! Easy. You see?
A: I knew.
B: This isn't the Central line.
A: What?
B: I said, this isn't the Central line. We're going the wrong way.
A: No … oh … wait a minute. You're right. We can get off at the next stop.
B: What stop is this?
A: Just a minute … I…
B: Can we ask someone?

A: No, no, it's all right. I…
B: Excuse me!
D: Yes?
B: How can we get to the British Museum?
D: Ah yes. It's easy.
B: Thank you, thank you.
D: Go upstairs and change to the Central line. Then go two stops, to Holborn station. The museum is there.
B: Thank you.
D: You're welcome.
A: Thank you.
B: Oh, stop it. You're just jealous.
A: No I'm not!

Unit 9

3.44

A: Here, look at this.
B: What … what is it?
A: It's an okapi. Have you ever seen one of these?
B: No, I haven't. It looks like … like a mixture of a horse, a dog and a zebra.
A: Mm. Yes. It's from the north part of the Congo. Africa. There aren't many okapis in the world now.
B: Have you been to Africa?
A: Yes, a long time ago. I've never seen this animal before. Not in real life.
B: Oh.
A: What about this one? Have you seen one of these?
B: Yes, I have. It's a lionfish, I think, from Australia?
A: Very good.
B: So … what now?
A: Well, have you used the Encyclopedia of Life website before?
B: No, I haven't.
A: OK. I want you to go on it and find information about one of these animals. Then write your report on one of these animals for tomorrow.
B: Is that the homework?
A: Yes, it is.
B: Thanks.
A: No problem. I'll go and see how the other students are doing.

3.48

1 When my sister got married she had a beautiful one on her hands.
2 I've got one on my arm, from when I was a soldier.
3 I've got one on my shoulder. It's a blue dolphin.
4 I'm a Maori from New Zealand. I've got a traditional 'Ta Moko' on my back.
5 Ugh. I hate them. My son's got a big star on his leg.

3.49

1 a car
2 two brothers
3 a friend from England
4 a computer
5 a big family
6 a friend with a tattoo

3.54

People started using buttons around 2000 BC in the south of Asia. The first ones were for decoration.

The first hats probably came from Asia, and were used to protect people from the sun and the rain. The earliest images of people in hats are from Greece in the year 500 BC.

The word sock comes from the Latin 'soccus', a type of ancient Roman shoe. But the first people to use socks were the Egyptians – in around 400 BC.

Clothes didn't have pockets until about 1500. Before then, people carried money and small items in bags.

People started wearing blue jeans in the 1860s in San Francisco. Originally people used them as thick protective trousers for work.

In 1917 a company called Keds in the United States invented the first sports shoes. These shoes were not all white like modern ones. They were black and brown, like other men's shoes at the time.

People started wearing T-shirts at the end of the 19th century. In 1939 clothes companies started printing words on T-shirts for promotion. They used the first one to advertise the film *The Wizard of Oz*.

3.55

1 **A:** What happened?
   B: Hello. You fell down.
   A: I fell down?
   B: Yes. But you're OK now.
   A: Oh ... My leg hurts.
   B: Don't worry, you haven't broken your leg.
   A: I've got an awful headache.
   B: Yes, that's normal.
   A: Where am I?
   B: In the ambulance, madam. We're going to the hospital.
   A: Oh ... OK. Can I have some water?
   B: Yes, of course. Here you are.

3.56

2 **A:** Excuse me, where's Dr Hathaway's office?
   B: Go straight on. It's the second door on the left.
   A: Thank you.
   C: Come in!
   A: Hello, er, Dr Hathaway?
   C: Yes, hello, Mr Fisher. What's the problem?
   A: Well, I have a terrible stomach ache.
   C: Really?
   A: But not now. It comes and goes.
   C: Hm. Can you sit down? Are you taking that medicine I gave you?
   A: Yes, I am.
   C: Maybe the medicine is too strong.

Unit 10

3.60

1 I'm interested in history so I'm going to visit the old bits of Malta. The churches, castles, museums and that kind of stuff.

3.61

2 I'm not here for tourism, I'm here for work. We're going to have a conference here next spring and I'm organising it.

3.62

3 We're here with the children, and they aren't going to want to see the cultural things. We're going to visit the water park and the beaches.

3.63

4 My friend and I love scuba diving. There are some amazing underwater caves here in Malta and we're going to swim in them.

3.64

5 We're going to get married there. We live in London but my girlfriend's family is Maltese. We're going to have a big party at a restaurant in the capital city. It's next to the sea and it's a great place for a wedding.

3.65

6 No, we're not going for tourism. We're making a television show about ancient Rome, and we're going to film some scenes in Malta because the architecture is so great.

3.66

7 I'm going to learn English there this summer. There are many English schools.

3.73

1 **A:** What did you do in class yesterday?
   B: We played a game.
   A: Really? What game?
   B: I can't remember the name. The teacher wrote some categories on the board.
   A: What do you mean, categories?
   B: Well, she wrote Animal, and City, and Verb and some other ones. Then she said a letter and we had to write a word for each category that begins with the letter.
   A: Oh. So ... for example ...
   B: For example she wrote S and we had to write an animal that begins with S ...
   A: Snake.
   B: Yeah, and a city ...
   A: San Francisco.
   B: Right, and that was the game. The team that finished first shouted "stop".
   A: Sounds fun.
   B: Yeah, it was fun.

3.74

2 In this game, you put several small objects, maybe around twenty, on the table and you cover them. Then you uncover the objects and let the people look at them for one minute. Then you cover the objects again. Each person writes down the things they remember. The person who remembers the most things wins.

3.75

3 OK, is everyone listening? Are you listening? Right, we're going to play a game. I'm thinking of a person, a famous person. You need to ask me questions to find out who it is. And I can only answer 'yes' or 'no'. So, for example, you ask, 'Are you a man?' and I answer, 'Yes, I am.' And you ask, 'Are you English?' and I answer 'No, I'm not.' And we continue. You can only ask a maximum of twenty questions to find out who I am. Ready? Who wants to ask the first question?

3.77

1 **A:** Hello, I'm your tour guide for the day. Is this your first time in Egypt?
   B: Yes, it is.
   A: What would you like to visit?
   B: Um ... I don't know. What do you suggest?
   A: We could see the pyramids. Everybody likes the pyramids.
   B: Oh, yes. Let's see the pyramids. When do they open?
   A: They open at 8 in the morning. They close at 4pm.
   B: OK.

3.78

2 **A:** And yes, so this is Red Square.
   B: Ooh, very nice. Where is the Kremlin?
   A: There, on the right. It's those buildings. We could go in and visit ...
   B: Are there long queues for tickets?
   A: Yes.
   B: Oh, no thanks then. We can walk around here, it's fine.

3.79

3 **A:** Welcome to Turkey. Have you visited Istanbul before?
   B: Yes, I have, but only for business. This is my first tourist visit.
   A: Oh, good. What would you like to see?
   B: I think it has to be the Hagia Sophia, don't you?
   A: Oh yes, of course. Why don't we go to your hotel first and you can leave your bags. Then we can go and see the sights.
   B: Good idea. Let's go.

Irregular verbs

Infinitive	Past simple	Past participle
be	was/were	been
beat	beat	beaten
become	became	become
begin	began	begun
bend	bent	bent
bet	bet	bet
bite	bit	bitten
blow	blew	blown
break	broke	broken
bring	brought /brɔːt/	brought /brɔːt/
build /bɪld/	built /bɪlt/	built /bɪlt/
burn	burnt/burned	burnt/burned
burst	burst	burst
buy /baɪ/	bought /bɔːt/	bought /bɔːt/
can	could /kʊd/	(been able)
catch	caught /kɔːt/	caught /kɔːt/
choose	chose	chosen
come	came	come
cost	cost	cost
cut	cut	cut
deal /diːl/	dealt /delt/	dealt /delt/
dig	dug	dug
do	did	done
draw	drew	drawn
dream	dreamt/dreamed	dreamt/dreamed
drink	drank	drunk
drive	drove	driven
eat	ate	eaten
fall	fell	fallen
feed	fed	fed
feel	felt	felt
fight	fought /fɔːt/	fought /fɔːt/
find	found	found
fly	flew	flown
forget	forgot	forgotten
forgive	forgave	forgiven
freeze	froze	frozen
get	got	got
give	gave	given
go	went	gone/been
grow	grew	grown
hang	hung/hanged	hung/hanged
have	had	had
hear	heard /hɜːd/	heard /hɜːd/
hide	hid	hidden
hit	hit	hit
hold	held	held
hurt /hɜːt/	hurt /hɜːt/	hurt /hɜːt/
keep	kept	kept
kneel	knelt/kneeled	knelt/kneeled
know	knew /njuː/	known
lay	laid	laid
lead	led	led
learn	learnt	learnt
leave	left	left
lend	lent	lent
let	let	let

Infinitive	Past simple	Past participle
lie	lay	lain
light	lit	lit
lose	lost	lost
make	made	made
mean	meant /ment/	meant /ment/
meet	met	met
must	had to	(had to)
pay	paid	paid
put	put	put
read	read /red/	read /red/
ride	rode	ridden
ring	rang	rung
rise	rose	risen
run	ran	run
say	said /sed/	said /sed/
see	saw /sɔː/	seen
sell	sold	sold
send	sent	sent
set	set	set
shake	shook	shaken
shine	shone	shone
shoot	shot	shot
show	showed	shown
shrink	shrank	shrunk
shut	shut	shut
sing	sang	sung
sink	sank	sunk
sit	sat	sat
sleep	slept	slept
slide	slid	slid
smell	smelt/smelled	smelt/smelled
speak	spoke	spoken
spell	spelt/spelled	spelt/spelled
spend	spent	spent
spill	spilt/spilled	spilt/spilled
split	split	split
spoil	spoilt/spoiled	spoilt/spoiled
spread	spread	spread
stand	stood	stood
steal	stole	stolen
stick	stuck	stuck
swear	swore	sworn
swell	swelled	swollen/swelled
swim	swam	swum
take	took /tʊk/	taken
teach	taught /tɔːt/	taught /tɔːt/
tear	tore	torn
tell	told	told
think	thought /θɔːt/	thought /θɔːt/
throw	threw	thrown
understand	understood	understood
wake	woke	woken
wear	wore /wɔː/	worn
win	won /wʌn/	won /wʌn/
write	wrote	written

Macmillan Education
Between Towns Road, Oxford OX4 3PP
A division of Macmillan Publishers Limited
Companies and representatives throughout the world

ISBN 978-0-230-03291-0

Original design by Barbara Mercer and Katie Stephens
Page layout by eMC Design Limited
Illustrated by Jonathan Burton, Matthew Hams, Celia Hart, Piers Sanford,
Peter Harper and eMC Design Limited
Picture research by Sally Cole, Perseverance Works Limited
Cover design by Barbara Mercer
Cover photos (front, spine, back): by permission of the Museum of the
History of Science, University of Oxford/Keiko Ikeuchi.

Authors' acknowledgements:
First and foremost we would like to thank Rafael Alarcon-Gaeta and the
editorial and design teams at Macmillan: Nick Sheard, Stephanie Parker,
Barbara Mercer, Stig Vatland, Sarah O'Driscoll, Claire Sparkes, Carole
Hughes, Penny Ashfield, Hazel Barrett and Georgina Gilbert. We would
also like to thank Jo Greig, Matt Kay and the rest of the marketing team.
There are of course many other people whose efforts have helped to make
a book that we are really proud of, in particular Robert Campbell, Rob
Metcalf and Matt Beesley for their work on the eWorkbook.
Lindsay would especially like to thank his family and friends for
encouraging him and putting up with him throughout the writing of this
book.
Kate would like to dedicate this book to Angus, Rhona and Maya for their
love and support and for surviving the experience.

The author and publishers would like to thank all the teachers and
consultants who have piloted and reviewed the material. Particular
thanks go to the following people: Andrea Córdova, Susana Flores
(Anglo Multimedia School of English, Haedo, Buenos Aires, Argentina);
Ma. Cristina Maggi, Ma. Cristina Buero de Chinton (Friends' School
of English, Adrogué, Buenos Aires, Argentina); Mirta Zampini, Aldana
Anchorena, Elizabeth Rainieri, Ma. Soledad D. Mangiarotti, Pamela
Sabrina Pecorelli (IECI, Haedo, Buenos Aires, Argentina); Alejandro Jorge
Listrani (Cultural Inglesa de Palermo, Ciudad Autónoma de Buenos Aires,
Argentina); Lilian Itzicovitch Leventhal (Potential/Colegio I.L.Peretz,
São Paulo, Brazil); Ana Maria Miranda (Cultura Inglesa Ribeirão Preto,
(Ribeirão Preto, Brazil); Magali de Moraes Menti (FACCAT – Escola
Municipal Lauro Rodrigues, Porto Alegre, Brazil); Simone Sarmento
(PUCRS, Porto Alegre, Brazil); Laura Lee Lehto (Cultura Inglesa,
Fortaleza, Brazil); Viviane Cristine Silva Grossklauss, Analice Sandovetti
(Cultura Inglesa Jundiaí, Jundiaí, Brazil); Celia Aguiar de Almeida
Costa (Cultura Inglesa de Juiz de Fora, Brazil); Corina Celia Machado
Correa (Associação Alumni – São Paulo, Brazil); Jane Godwin (The
Four, São Carlos, Brazil); Caroline Toubia (The Holy Family School,
Jesuite, Egypt); Amany Shawkey, Heidi Omara (Macmillan Publishers
Ltd, Egypt) Caroline Franz , Dana Jelinkova (MVHS Muenchner
Volkshochschule, Munich, Germany); Irene Rodriguez, Haydee Gutierrez
Palafox, Antonio Morales de la Barrera, Javier Ramos de Hoyos (The
Anglo Mexican Foundation, Mexico City, Mexico); Viviana Caruso
de Curtius (freelance author and consultant, Mexico City, Mexico);
Emma Dominguez (Academic Studies Manager, The Anglo Mexican
Foundation, Mexico City, Mexico); Katarzyna Rogalińska-Gajewska
(Archibald, Warsaw, Poland); Małgorzata Woźniak, Dorota Pachwicewicz,
Agnieszka Kilanowska (Centrum Językowe 'Euroclub', Gdańsk, Poland);
Fabiola Georgiana Hosu (Little London School and Nursery School,

Dimitrie Cantemir University, Bucharest, Romania); Lydia B. Korzheva
(Diplomatic Academy, Moscow, Russia); Ludmila A. Pokrovskaya (Russian
Academy of Foreign Trade, Moscow, Russia); Olga S. Petrischeva
(Moscow State University of International Relations, Moscow,
Russia); Albina Valieva (The International Language School 'Denis
School', Moscow, Russia); Karen Dyer, Cathy Harris, Frank Hodgkins
(International House, Madrid, Spain); Carlos Trueba (E.O.I. Villaverde,
Madrid, Spain); Patricia Plaza Arregui (E.O.I. Malaga, Spain); Maria
Esther Álvarez Rico (E.O.I. Sagunto, Valencia, Spain); Burcu Tezcan Ünal
(Bilgi University, Istanbul, Turkey); Dr. F. Ilke Buyukduman (Ozyegin
University, Istanbul, Turkey); Sarah Shaw (The British Council, Chiang
Mai, Thailand); Aomboon Burutphakdee (Payap University, Chiang Mai,
Thailand); Nattinee Khueansri (Payap University, Chiang Mai, Thailand);
Claudia Edwards (London School of English, London, UK); Sally Jones
(Regent Oxford, Oxford, UK); Katherine Griggs (Community English
School, Oxfordshire Adult Learning, Oxford, UK)

A special thank you to Jackie Halsall, Sarah Paterson and all the staff and
students at Eckersley, Oxford and Regent, Oxford for all their help with
Global voices.

The authors and publishers would like to thank the following for
providing information about themselves to be included in the book:
Peter Menzel, Alan Hammans, Miguel Angel Nieto Baños, Laura Clunie.

The authors and publishers would like to thank the following for
permission to reproduce their photographs:

AKG Images pp130(tl), 130(bl), AKG-images/E. Lessing p130(m);
Alamy/Arco Images GmbH p102(bl), Alamy/J.Arnold Images pp18,
123(r), Alamy/M.Bassett p47(tl), Alamy/R.Bird p43(t), Alamy/J.Birdsall
p109(tmr), Alamy/F. Camhi p126(l), Alamy/W.Connett p92, Alamy/R.
Cummins p35(b), Alamy/M. Dwyer p24, Alamy/T. Eckert p37(m),
Alamy/J. Fernandez p104(b), Alamy/Focus Japan p115(r), Alamy/United
Archives GmbH p31(ml), Alamy/T.Foster p43(tm), Alamy/A. Fox
p23(mb), Alamy/D. R. Frazier Photolibrary, Inc. p90 Alamy/T.Gander
p13(mr), Alamy/G.Gay pp11(tl), 109(tl), 109(rtm), Alamy/E. Gerald pp21,
58(br inset), Alamy/D.Gowans p33(t), Alamy Robert Harding Picture
Library Ltd p123(ml), Alamy/A.Holt p116(tr), Alamy/Jam World Images
p116(tm), Alamy/D.Jenkins p36(tm), Alamy/H.Jones p116(b), Alamy/
Lebrecht Music and Arts Photo Library p121(r), Alamy/S.May p11(tr),
Alamy/R. McGinnis p84(r), Alamy/Pictorial Press Ltd p22(bl), Alamy/
Picture Partners p74(ml), Alamy/The Print Collector p130(mr), Alamy/
Profimedia International s.r.o. p102(br), Alamy/PSL Images p62(mr),
Alamy/Bert de Ruiter p26(ml), Alamy/H. Rogers p25(l), Alamy/A.
Segre p13(tl), Alamy/P. Scholey p116(m), Alamy/P.Springett p34(br),
Alamy/J.Sylvester p43(b), Alamy/TravelStock Collection/H.Sykes p33(b),
Alamy/Trinity Mirror/Mirrorpix p36(bm), Alamy/A. Kowalsky p11(br),
Alamy/G.Wrona p71(b); **Ancient Art & Architecture**/C.M.Dixon
p37; **Bananastock** pp67, 118(ml), 118(mr); **Miguel Angel Nieto
Baños** pp103(mr), 103(b); **Brand X** pp12(l), 23(m), 36(tl), 44(g,k),
90(bl), 118(tl,m,bl,bm); **Comstock** p44(c), 44(d); **Corbis**/M.Altmann
p37(mb), Corbis/Atlantide Phototravel p62(ml), Corbis/A. Benedetti
p112, Corbis/E.Bock p82(tr), Corbis/D.Brabyn p58(bm inset), Corbis/P.
Björkegren/Etsa p82(tl), Corbis/W. Perry Conway/p36(br), Corbis/R.
Dowling p84(m), Corbis/ The Gallery Collection p130(tm), Corbis/R.
Jack p31(b), Corbis/ J. Roberts p37(m), Corbis/E.Kashi p74(tl), Corbis/M.
Nelson/EPA p71(mr), Corbis/C.Platiau p79(b), Corbis/B.Rondel p8(bl),
Corbis/ Robert Sciarrino/Star Ledger p126(tr), Corbis/R. Schultz p36(tr),
Corbis/B.Vogel p126(br), Corbis/R.Weir p32, Corbis/S.Westmorland
p102(tl); **Corbis RF** pp23(tm), 28, 35(t), 44(I,g), 46(1,3,4,6,10,11), 90(mr),
97(suitcase,passport), 118(tm,tr); **CS Media,** media@couchsurfing.com.
p45(t); **Digital Vision** p47(br), 46(1), 85(t), 90(ml); **By kind permission
of Encyclopedia of Life** p102 (logo); **Fotolibra**/El-Louise Potgieter
p47(tmr), Fotolibra/S.J.Young p20(r), Fotolibra/R.Down p129(r); **Greater
Manchester Passenger Transport Executive** p98; **Homeless World
Cup** http://www.homelessworldcup.org p119; **John Frost Newspapers/**
The Washington Post p80(b);**Getty images** /AFP p62(r), Getty/Arabian
Eye p30, Getty/Archive Holdings Inc./Hulton Archive p55,Getty/Angelo
Cavali p50(r), Getty/D.K images/C.Stowers p93(t), Getty/D.K.Images
p109(tr), Getty/Gallo Images/Travel Ink p116(mr), Getty/Jonathan

Kirn p97(tl), Getty/National Geographic p84(l), Getty Images News p59, Getty Images Publicity p115(m), Getty/Photographers Choice pp10, 12(r), Getty/Photonica pp57(tr), 83, 109(br), Getty/S. Pitamitz p50(m), Getty/Retrofile p66(bl), Getty/Riser pp38(tr), p50(l), 66(tr), 82(ml), 86(l), Getty/Robert Harding World Imagery p128(tr), Getty/Stone pp14(mr), 23(t), 45(b), 56(bl), 56(br), 57(tm), 66(ml), 82(b), p132, 109(bmr), 110(ml), Getty/Taxi pp38(bl), 66(mr), Getty/Uppercut Images p57(tml), Getty/The Image Bank pp23(b), 26(r), 38(br) 57(tl), 58(b), 106(l), 120(r), p129(m), Getty/Taxi Japan p128(br), Getty/Time & Life Pictures pp6(ml), 56(t); **Alan Hammans** p85(b); **Image Source** pp7, 9(br), 46(7),76, 90(t); **Impact Photos**/P.Menzel pp 49(bl, br), 134(t, b); **Joshua Tree Photography** pp 13(portraits), 57(m,b), 58(portraits),73(t),94, 97(bl,tr,br), 131(bl,br); **Lebrecht Music Collection**/T. Kenton p31(br); **Lonely Planet**/B.Cruickshank p19, Lonely Planet/A.Blomqvist p106(r), Lonely Planet/D.Tomlinson p127(r); **Macmillan Publishers Ltd** p114(br), Macmillan Publishers Ltd/P.Bricknell pp114(ml), 114(bl), Macmillan Publishers Ltd/Haddon Davies pp44(f), 46(12), Macmillan Publishers Ltd/Dean Ryan/Rob Judges p44(e), Macmillan Publishers Ltd/D.Tolley pp 44(9),46(13),114(tr),114(tl); **Masterfile**/G.Grenier p68(r), Masterfile/M.Mahovlich p74(tr), Masterfile/H.Vu p74(mr); **Nature pl**/Aflo p6(b), Nature pl/J.Walker p11(bl); **PA**/L.MacDougal/The Canadian Press p43(bm); **Panos Pictures**/R.Jones p104(tl); **Photoalto** pp90(m), 93(b),118(br); **Photodisc** pp44(a,b,h,j),52; **Photographers Direct**/O.Noel p71(tr), Photographers Direct/Thierry Dehesdin p121(l); **Photolibrary**/Esbin-Anderson p36(bl), Photolibrary/The British Library p78(tl), Photolibrary/Cuboimages p116(tl), Photolibrary/Y. Depollas p64, Photolibrary/N.Emmerson p14(r), Photolibrary/V.Ernst p109(tml), Photolibrary/M.Fogden p103(t), Photolibrary/P.Harrison p128(l), Photolibrary/Gavin Hellier p123(L), Photolibrary/HIRB p14(l), Photolibrary/P. Jiropas p128(mr), Photolibrary/J.Lee p47(tr), Photolibrary/L. Lepre p20(l), Photolibrary/Y.Liu p86(ml), Photolibrary/A. Mares-Manton p38(tl), Photolibrary/D. Marsden p127(l), Photolibrary/Mary Inc p107, Photolibrary/B.Morandi p106(m), Photolibrary/D. Pitcher p127(m), Photolibrary/M. Polverelli p129(l), Photolibrary/J. Raga p123(mr), Photolibrary/J-C&D, Pratt/Photononstop p115(l), Photolibrary/IPS Photo Index p47(tml), Photolibrary/S. Raphael p49(t), Photolibrary/S. Raymer p34(ml), Photolibrary/G. Rohman p126(mr), Photolibrary/J. Sheagren p37(tm), Photolibrary/J. Tack p62(l), Photolibrary/Vidler p71(ml), Photolibrary/R. Waldkirch p26(mr), Photolibrary/A. Weller p26(l), Photolibrary/C. & M. Werner p66(tl); **By kind permission of Rhona Barclay Pickering** p73(b); **Plainpicture**/Hasengold p86(mr); **Reuters**/H. New p110(l); **Still Pictures**/C. Blumenstein p102(tr); **Rex Features** p86(r), Rex/D Cooper p31(tm), Rex/Design Pics Inc p82(tml), Rex/J.Downing p70,Rex/Everett Collection pp80(t), 81(b), 130(tr), Rex/Image Source p120(l), Rex/ITV p58(bl, inset), Rex/B.Jones p9(t), Rex/T. Larkin p31(tr), Rex/J.Lyons p66(br), Rex/J. McCauley p105, Rex/J. Ritola p14(ml); **Science Photo Library**/P. Menzel p48, Science Photo Library/BSIP,LA p110(mr), Science Photo Library/M.Donne p110(r); **Stockbyte** pp6(tr), 97(umbrella),114(mr), 116; **Studio 8** p46(8); **Superstock** p13(tr); **Topfoto** pp78(bl),(br), p79(t), Topfoto/HIP p37(t),Topfoto/The Granger Collection pp68(m), 130(ml), Topfoto/Image Works p81(t), Topfoto/UPPA p130(br); By kind permission of United World Tourism Organization/Centro Español de Derechos Reprográficos p70(l); **Medio Images Vidalatina** p 40; **The Kobal Collection**/ Trial by Fire p54; **Almanac Image** courtesy of the South Asian Division of the Library of Congress, p25(r).

Commissioned photography by **Dean Ryan** pp22(t),108; **Joshua Tree Photography** pp15, 39,63,75,87.

The author and publishers are grateful for permission to reprint the following copyright material: The National Post Company for an extract adapted from 'Unusual places to lay down your weary head' National Post, 10 May 2007 www.canada.com, material reprinted with the express permission of The National Post Company, a Canwest Partnership; Homeless World Cup Organisation for extracts from 'From the Bottle to the Cup', 6 Feb 2008; 'A ball can change the world'; and 'Edinburgh 2005 – Player Quotes': Ricardo Arma, Captain Italy, Homeless World Cup Champions; and Dermot Haverty, Captain, Ireland, © www.homelessworldcup.org.

These materials may contain links for third party websites. We have no control over, and are not responsible for, the contents of such third party websites. Please use care when accessing them.

Although we have tried to trace and contact copyright holders before publication, in some cases this has not been possible. If contacted we will be pleased to rectify any errors or omissions at the earliest opportunity.

Printed in Thailand

2014 2013 2012
11 10 9 8